1 MONTH OF
FREE
READING

at

www.ForgottenBooks.com

By purchasing this book you are eligible for one month membership to ForgottenBooks.com, giving you unlimited access to our entire collection of over 1,000,000 titles via our web site and mobile apps.

To claim your free month visit:
www.forgottenbooks.com/free799655

ISBN 978-0-483-99045-6
PIBN 10799655

v

❖ The Treasury. ❖

A COMPANION TUNE BOOK

TO

"PSALMS & HYMNS FOR SCHOOL & HOME."

COMPILED AND EDITED BY

JOSEPH B. MEAD.

REVISED AND ENLARGED.

Embodying the improvements introduced in the Congregational
Edition of THE TREASURY,
And including the supplementary Tunes 423—466.

₊ The Profits are annually distributed among the Widows and Orphans of
Baptist Ministers and Missionaries.

London:

PUBLISHED BY THE TRUSTEES, 25, BOUVERIE STREET,
FLEET STREET, E.C.

R. 3—1,250—10,250.

GEORGE WILSON, MUSIC AND GENERAL PRINTER,
67b, TURNMILL STREET, LONDON, E.C.

EDITOR'S PREFACE.

"THE TREASURY" is primarily a Companion Tune Book to "Psalms and Hymns for School and Home," and in the alphabetical index of the hymns, one or more suitable tunes are given for each hymn in the Collection. Advantage has been taken of the opportunity to add a few tunes,* making further provision for various hymns in "Psalms and Hymns for Public, Social and Private Worship," beyond that contained in the Tune Books generally used by our denomination ; also in addition to the companion tunes, "THE TREASURY" includes about forty leading favourites for anniversary and other hymns,† beyond those found in the hymn book.

The aim throughout has been to utilize and concentrate the excellences of all standard collections, and to "hold fast that which is good," rather than to add to the volume of new and untested music. Established names have not been altered, the best familiar arrangements have been selected, and in these no variations of harmony have been made, excepting when an occasional amendment has been needed to secure grammatical correctness. For many of the peculiar metres the choice of tunes is necessarily restricted ; for the metres more generally used, the provision made is most ample, and it is hoped that the tunes selected will be found "capable of embodying the purest thoughts and noblest aspirations of both religion and art," no pains or expense having been spared to compile a book adequately meeting the varied requirements of our " Schools and Homes."

Every attention has been paid in the setting, to fix the tune that most fully expresses the "eloquence of the hymn," but whenever an alternative tune seems equally suitable, nothing is easier than to adopt it. When a hymn is definitely associated with a tune, it is strongly recommended, as a rule, not to put asunder that which has thus been joined together, it being preferable that each hymn should have its inalienable tune.

The system adopted in the omission of time signatures, the arrangement of bars and double bars, the length of the commencing and terminal notes, and the repetition of the clef signatures, have all been the result of careful consideration, and it is believed that greatly increased steadiness and confidence will be secured by taking all tunes in strict time exactly as written. Although the tunes are generally printed in the modern notation, it is not intended they should be sung more rapidly than if printed in minims and semibreves. The subject of each hymn will indicate to the reverent mind the proper speed of its tune, and a just medium will be preserved between a careless drawl and an unseemly haste, both equally prejudicial to the devout spirit that should characterize our worship.

---

* Almost all of these were included in the Congregational Edition of "THE TREASURY" when published in 1887.

† All these Hymns are included in the supplement added in 1892.

Without any exception, all the permissions requested have been granted, and the arduous labour involved in the undertaking has been greatly lightened by the Christian courtesy and hearty willingness with which friends on all hands have placed their accumulated treasures at our disposal, a specially pleasing trait being the fraternal sympathy manifested by numerous friends in the Church of England, and the cordial terms by which their consent has been given.

I am exclusively responsible for the selection and setting, with all details and arrangements adopted ; but in the important work of preparing for the press and correction of proofs I have been fortunate in the valued co-operation of Dr. Arthur S. Holloway, whose long experience and high professional ability give the fullest assurance of technical correctness throughout.

"The saints, in prayer, appear as one," and "THE TREASURY" is an offering dedicated to GOD, in the hope that this labour of love may be owned by Him to an increase of communion and oneness in our methods of presenting our sacrifice of praise at His mercy-seat.

May, 1883.   JOSEPH B. MEAD.

PREFACE TO THE REVISED EDITION.

The Trustees of "Psalms and Hymns" having acquired "THE TREASURY," and published a "Congregational Edition" of the work, in which various improvements have been introduced, have pleasure in issuing a revision of the "School and Home Edition," in which all such emendations are embodied. In many instances these are very slight ; in others, they are of importance ; while a few tunes—Nos. 27, 38, 59, 77, 98, 131, 171, 230, 245, and 260—have been reset in other keys.

An * in the heading denotes those in which changes have been made. The inconvenience of varying arrangements of one tune will be temporary, while the advantages of both editions of "THE TREASURY" being uniform in the tunes common to both, are permanent.

25, Bouverie Street,
March, 1888.

Every effort has been made to obtain permission from their composers or proprietors for the use of the copyright tunes in this Collection, and to acknowledge the same. The Trustees have endeavoured to trace the source of every tune selected, but in a very few instances their attempts to communicate with writers have failed, or they have been unable to obtain definite information : should they thus have inadvertently infringed any copyright, they offer every apology, and will gladly make any necessary rectification in future editions.

TABLE OF ACKNOWLEDGMENTS.

REV. HENRY ALLON, D.D., for Nos. 132, 270, 343, 347, and 366, from "The Congregational Psalmist," etc.

THE RIGHT REV. E. H. BICKERSTETH, D.D., Bishop of Exeter, for arrangements of Nos. 67, 254, and 429, from "The Hymnal Companion."

REV. W. J. BLEW, M.A., for Nos. 10, 191, 216, 248, and 311, by DR. GAUNTLETT, from "Church Hymn and Tune Book."

THE PROPRIETORS OF "THE BRISTOL TUNE BOOK," for Nos. 17, 29, 52, 109, 144, 192, 235, 284, 292, 312, and 417.

MESSRS. BROWN & CO., for No. 258, from "The Sarum Hymnal."

REV. R. R. CHOPE, B.A., for Nos. 138 and 143, from "The Congregational Hymn and Tune Book."

MESSRS. ROBERT COCKS & CO., for No. 466.

MR. G. T. CONGREVE, for arrangements of Nos. 301, 324, and 389, from "Gems of Song."

THE COMPILERS OF "CONGREGATIONAL CHURCH MUSIC," for Nos. 2, 7, 15, 41, 47, 49, 234, 291, and 332.

MESSRS. JOHN HADDON & CO., for Nos. 33, 46, 87, 101, 107, 111, 154, 169, 182, 246, 289, 318, and 378, from "The Psalmist."

THE PROPRIETORS OF "HYMNS ANCIENT AND MODERN," for Nos. 20, 197, 232, 262, 280, 337, 355, 356, 381, 397, 428, and 465.

MR. W. MACK, for Nos. 9, 28, 69, 115, 124, 137, 244, 277, 442, and 453, from "Tunes and Chants for Home and School."

THE PROPRIETORS OF "THE METHODIST SUNDAY SCHOOL TUNE BOOK," for Nos. 44, 66, 81, 82, 123, 130, 227, 322, and 370; and arrangements of Nos. 147 and 249.

MESSRS. MORGAN & SCOTT, for Nos. 229, 349, and 382.

MESSRS. JAMES NISBET & CO., for Nos. 179, 203, 213, 308, 317, and 431, from "Church Praise."

MESSRS. NOVELLO, EWER, & CO., for Nos. 103, 149, 231, 281, 313, 426, 449, and 456; and arrangements of Nos. 27 and 38.

THE PROPRIETORS OF "THE SACRED MELODIST," for No. 385.

THE PROPRIETORS OF "THE SCHOOL HYMNAL," for Nos. 31, 34, 70, 125, 194, 212, 221, 222, 283, 287, and 325.

THE SUNDAY SCHOOL UNION, for Nos. 21, 63, 217, 256, 288, 303, 309, 344, 391, and 399.

REV. H. A. WALKER, for No. 37, from "The St. Albans' Tune Book."

THE WESLEYAN SUNDAY SCHOOL UNION, for No. 463.

MR. JOHN ADCOCK, for Nos. 184, 243, 360, and 434.

MR. JOSEPH BARNBY, for No. 461.

MR. W. BEST, for No. 335.

REV. W. BLOW, for No. 333.

MR. JOSIAH BOOTH, for No. 445.

REV. R. BROWN BORTHWICK, for No. 51.

MR. A. H. BROWN, for Nos. 225 and 295.

REV. DR. BULLINGER, for Nos. 278, 331, and 372; and Nos. 164 and 363, written expressly for this work.

MESSRS. BURNS & OATES, Limited, for No. 386.

MR. H. ELLIOT BUTTON, for No. 436.

Mr A. J. Caldicott, Mus. Bac., for No. 457.
Mr. J. Baptiste Calkin, for No. 452.
Rev. E. S. Carter, for Nos. 286 and 290.
Mr. S. Clarke, for No. 279.
Rev. H. A. Crosbie, for Nos. 142, 207, 297.
Messrs. J. Curwen & Sons, for No. 257.
Mr. C. Darnton, for No. 395.
Mr. Andrew Deakin, for No. 199.
Mr. Edwin Drewett, for No. 441.
Mr. Frederick Dykes, for No. 424.
Mr. J. W. Elliott, for No. 198.
Sir G. J. Elvey, for No. 266.
Mr. W. C. Filby, for Nos. 226 and 359.
Lady Victoria Freke, for No. 354.
Mrs. Gauntlett, for Nos. 18, 23, 121, and 304.
Mr. Samuel Gee, for No. 438.
Mr. John Guest, for No. 371.
Mr. Thomas S. Guest, for No. 228.
Miss F. R. Havergal, for No. 148.
Rev. L. G. Hayne, Mus. Doc., for No. 163.
Mr. Henri C. Hemy, for Nos. 67, 161, 387, and 394.
Dr. Henry Hiles, for No. 119.
Messrs. Hodder & Stoughton, for No. 136.
Dr. Arthur S. Holloway, for Nos. 162 and 214.
Mr. H. J. E. Holmes, for No. 460.
Dr. E. J. Hopkins, for Nos. 170 and 435.
Mr. R. Jackson, for Nos. 205 and 454.
Dr. T. R. G. Jozé, for No. 432.
Mr. W. H. Jude, for No. 455.
Mr. Henry Lahee, for No. 190.
Mr. James Langran, Mus. Bac., for No. 357.
Mr. H. J. Leslie, for No. 444.
Mr. G. Lomas, Mus. Bac., for Nos. 165 and 177.
Mr. F. C. Maker, for Nos. 439 and 458; and Nos. 186 and 187; written expressly
  for this work.
Dr. A. H. Mann, for No. 195.
Rev. T. R. Matthews, for Nos. 135, 167, 265, and 446.
Mr. J. H. Maunder, for Nos. 440 and 464.
Mr. Ernest J. Mead, for Nos. 268 and 369.
Rev. W. Mercer, for No. 269.
Mr. A. B. Merrick, for No. 178.
Messrs. Metzler & Co., for Nos. 245 and 346.
Messrs. R. Mills & Sons, for No. 410.
Mr. R. S. Newman, for No. 75.
Mr. Clement H. Perrot, for No. 437.
Mr. C. W. Poole, for No. 92.
Rev. C. C. Scholefield, for No. 430.
Rev. Canon Seymour, Dublin, for No. 134.
Messrs. Shaw & Co., for No. 73.
Mr. Samuel Smith, for No. 150.
Mr. W. A. Smith, for No. 80.
Sir Robert P. Stewart, Mus. Doc., for arrangements of Nos. 131 and 230.
Mr. Elliot Stock, for No. 139.
Mrs. Streatfield, for No. 6.
Sir Arthur Sullivan, Mus. Doc., for Nos. 76, 174, 176, 329, and 406.
Mr. B. Taylor, for No. 367.
Mr. G. B. Thackwray, for No. 275.
Mr. Berthold Tours, for No. 433.
The Representatives of the late Mr. Troyte, per Rev. C. S. Bere, for
  Nos. 404 and 418.
Miss Alice S. Tucker, for No. 459.
Mr. J. Turle, for No. 59.
Mr. C. J. Vincent, Junr., for No. 443.
Mr. J. Walch, for Nos. 54 and 210.
The Representatives of Dr. Wesley, for No. 196.
Mr. W. Wilcox, for No. 181.
Mr. Joseph Williams, for No. 264.

ALPHABETICAL INDEX OF TUNES.

	NO.		NO.		NO.
A crowd fills the	344	Brookfield	275	Easter Hymn	250
A crown for the young	375	Budleigh	132	Echo Song	172
Agatha	166	Bullinger	278	Eden	88
Agnus Dei	333	Bury St. Edmunds	167	Eglon	256
Alcock's Chant	407	Byzantium	27	Eisenach	89
Aldrich's Chant	408			Ellacombe	74
Alpha	444	Calvary	305	Ellers	354
Alsace	427	Cambridge	3	Ellingham	237
Alstone	428	Canaan	324	Elmhurst	441
Amaranth	161	Canonbury	86	Emmeline	124
Angel Voices	281	Cape Town	233	Ems	402
Angelic Host	315	Carbrooke	445	Endsleigh	369
Angel's Story	195	Carlisle	4	Epiphany Hymn	377
Angelus	83	Cassel	253	Erastus	394
Anniversary	60	Castle Rising	426	Ernan	90
Anniversary Song	112	Celeste	336	Evan	30
Ariel	180	Chenies	446	Evangelist	31
Arnolds	24	Chester	235	Even me	299
Ascension	18	Chichester	318	Evening Hymn	91
Ashburton	454	Children of Jerusalem	249	Evensong (6.5.)	134
Assurance	19	Children's Jubilee	63	Evensong (8.7.)	312
Athens	376	Children's Voices	170	Eventide	355
At the Cross there's	183	Christ arose	153	Ewing	202
Audite Audientes me	73	Christine	160	Exeter	173
Augustine	1	Christmas Bells	82		
Auld Lang Syne	70	Christmas Hymn	263	Fairford	448
Aurelia	196	Civitas Dei	457	Farrant	32
Austria	314	Clarabella	28	Fleury	145
Autumn	188	Clarion	345	Florence	319
Aylesbury	359	Columbia	395	Follow Me	221
		Come, let us all unite	274	Foundation	387
Barton	189	Come to the Saviour	168	Franconia (S.M.)	5
Baun	289	Come unto Me	197	Franconia (6.5.)	139
Beacon	325	Compassion	343	Friburg	340
Beautiful home of	268	Consolator	279		
Beautiful stream	373	Coppet	146	Galilee	455
Beautiful stream	463	Creation	113	Gawthorpe	181
Bedford	25	Crosby	151	German Hymn	238
Beethoven	84	Crotch's Chant	410	Gibraltar	92
Belfield	372			Glory	61
Bellevue	226	Dalehurst	29	Glory	62
Belmont	26	Danbury	164	God bless the Prince	
Beneath the Cross	229	Darwells	171	of Wales	466
Benedicite	303	Day by Day	290	Gounod	313
Benediction	316	Day of rest	198	Greenland	203
Benevento	261	Dear Saviour, we	388	Greenwood	423
Benignus	214	Dedham	199		
Bethany	317	Derby	133	Handel's Chant	412
Beulah	129	Deva	435	Hanford	329
Blandford	154	Diademata	20	Hanover	364
Bluntisham	117	Dijon	236	Hark, hark, my soul	380
Boston	85	Dismissal	306	Harlington	201
Boyce's Chant	409	Dix	254	Hart's	239
Braylesford	304	Dolomite Chant	429	Harvest	125
Brightly beams our	300	Doversdale	87	Harwich	120
Brighton	2	Dunkirk	200	Havannah	33
Brockley	155	Dupuis' Chant	411	Haverstock	251

	NO.
Haydn	147
Heaven	64
Heaven, sweet heaven	464
Heber	204
Henley's Chant	413
Hereford	323
Hermas	148
Holley	93
Hollingside	262
Holstein	34
Home, sweet home	389
Honidon	265
Honiton	94
Horsley	35
Hosanna	121
Hosanna we sing	465
Houghton	366
How many sheep	223
How sweet is the Bible	371
Humility	335
Hursley	95
I am Jesus' little friend	272
I have a Saviour	390
I love the Name	217
I love to tell the Story	215
I will arise	420
If I come to Jesus	140
In the highways	398
Indiana	131
Inglewhite	169
Innocents	240
Intercession	179
Invitation	439
Iona	264
Irene	430
Irish	36
It passeth knowledge	462
Jesus is our Shepherd	141
Jesus, keep me near	193
Jesus, little children	277
Jesus loves me	252
Joyful	230
Joyfully, joyfully	365
Just as I am	334
Kiel	241
Knocking	271
Lacrymæ	231
Lætitia	37
Land of Rest	75
Langton	6
Langdon's Chant	414
Laudamus	178
Lausanne	291
Lead me to Jesus	353
Leslie	442
Listen ! the Master	327
London New	38
Loudon	7
Love one another	392
Lucerne	292
Luther's Chant	96
Lux Mundi	449

	NO.
Lymington	205
Lyndhurst	431
Mainzer	97
Manchester	39
Mannheim	307
Manoah	40
March of Life	348
Mariners'	293
Marlborough	378
Marlow	41
Martyrdom	42
Melcombe	98
Mendelssohn	450
Miles' Lane	43
Missionary	206
Monmouth	339
Montgomery	99
Morden	182
Morning Hymn	100
Morning Star	257
Mornington's Chant	415
Moscow	156
Mossleigh	207
Mount Ephraim	8
Mount St. Bernard	162
Mountmellick	432
Munich	208
Musical Dream	419
Nain	126
Nassau	255
National Anthem	157
Nativity	284
Nazareth	44
Neapolis	101
Nearer Home	21
Nearer to Thee	130
Newark	222
Newhaven	158
Newport	283
New York	209
Nicæa	397
Nocturne	269
Noël	76
North Coates	135
Nottingham	242
Oasis	165
O Christian, awake	391
O happy day	116
O Paradise	67
O Paradise	68
O sing to the Lord	123
O think of the home	342
Oldenburg	384
Old Hundredth	102
Old Winchester	45
Olivet	159
Ombersley	103
On to the conflict	368
One more day's work	186
One more day's work	187
Our Sabbath Song	322
Palestine	77

	NO.
Parkholme	438
Pass me not	282
Pater Omnium	460
Patmos	360
Pax Dei	356
Percy	243
Philippi	46
Pilgrimage	194
Pilgrims	381
Pilgrim Song	433
Praise	328
Prospect	78
Pulchra	244
Redemption	66
Redhead	245
Regent Square	308
Rejoice and be glad	382
Requiem	258
Resignation	330
Rest	385
Return, O wanderer	72
Reynold's Chant	417
Richmond	47
Ring the bells of heav'n	374
Robinson's Chant	416
Rockingham	104
Rothbury	440
Rousseau	309
Ruth	150
Rutherford	451
Sacrifice	190
Safe Home	174
Safe in the Arms	219
St. Agnes (10s.)	357
St. Agnes (C.M.)	424
St. Agnes (7s.)	459
St. Alphege (7.6.7.6.)	191
St. Alphege (7.6.8.6.)	216
St. Anatolius	225
St. Ann's	48
St. Austin	9
St. Cecilia	163
St. Cephas	142
St. Christopher	458
St. Clothilde	136
St. Faith	396
St. George	10
St. George's (Bolton)	210
St. George's (Windsor)	266
St. Gertrude	149
St. Helen	294
St. Hilda	122
St. James	49
St. John	175
St. Jude	137
St. Lambert	138
St. Luke	386
St. Mabyn	295
St. Magnus	50
St. Mary Magdalene	143
St. Matthew	79
St. Matthias	337
St. Michael	11
St. Patrick	367

	NO.
St. Peter	51
St. Philip	192
St. Saviour	52
St. Stephen	53
St. Theodulph	211
St. Werburgh	310
St. Winifred	69
Salem	403
Salome	379
Samson	105
Samuel	176
Sanctus	405
Sardis	296
Saviour, Thy dying love	128
Savoy Chapel	452
Sawley	54
Schubert	212
Sefton	297
Selattyn	331
Seraphim	352
Serenity	12
Shadows	270
Shall we gather	302
Shall we meet	301
Sharon	298
Shiloh (Endsleigh)	213
Shirland	13
Shoreham	332
Silchester	14
Silksworth	443
Simeon	106
Sing with a tuneful	224
So near to the kingdom	393
Solicitude	246
Solomon	55
Sound the battle cry	118
Sound the loud timbrel	370
Sowing the seed	347
Spain	259
Spes Celestis	80

	NO.
Spohr	65
Springtime	406
Stand up for Jesus	115
Star of Peace	288
Stella	338
Stephanos	280
Strike for victory	152
Sumus Tibi	436
Sweet hour of prayer	114
Sweet Sabbath School	71
Sympathy	425
Syria	267
Tabor	276
Tallis	56
Tamerton	15
Te Deum Laudamus	422
Tell me the old, old	218
Tenterden	363
The better land	346
The golden chain	447
The golden rule	184
The good old way	361
The Master is come	350
The sweetest name	287
The wandering sheep	22
Theodora	247
There is a green hill	81
There is a holy City	453
There is life for a look	400
There is life for a look	401
There's a beautiful land	399
There's a beautiful land [on high	341
Thou didst leave Thy	349
Tierney	23
Tiverton	57
Toulon	358
Tours	456
Trevu	227

	NO.
Trinitas	437
Triumph	311
Tromso	273
Troyte's Chant (No. 1)	418
Troyte's Chant (No. 2)	404
Tuam	17
Tytherton	16
University College	248
Valentia	127
Veni Domine Jesu	461
Verbum Pacis	177
Vesper	320
Vespers	144
Vigilate	232
Vital Spark	421
Wandsworth	107
Wanswell	234
Warrington	108
Warwick	58
We are marching on	383
We plough the fields	220
Wells	260
Westminster	59
What a friend	321
When He cometh	285
Whitburn	109
Whither, pilgrims	326
Wiclif	228
Winchcombe	119
Winchester	110
Woodbrook	434
Woolstanton	111
Work for the night	185
Wreford	286
Yet there is room	351
Yorkshire	362

METRICAL INDEX.

Short Metres.

6.6.8.6.	NO.
Augustine	1
Brighton	2
Cambridge	3
Carlisle	4
Franconia	5
Greenwood	423
Langton	6
Loudon	7
Mount Ephraim	8
St. Austin	9
St. George	10
St. Michael	11
Serenity	12
Shirland	13
Silchester	14
Tamerton	15
Tuam	17
Tytherton	16

6.6.8.6. D.

Ascension	18
Assurance	19
Diademata	20
Nearer Home	21
The wandering sheep	22
Tierney	23

Common Metres.

8.6.8.6.

Arnolds	24
Bedford	25
Belmont	26
Byzantium	27
Clarabella	28
Dalehurst	29
Evan	30
Evangelist	31
Farrant	32
Havannah	33
Holstein	34
Horsley	35
Irish	36
Lætitia	37
London (New)	38
Manchester	39
Manoah	40
Marlow	41
Martyrdom	42
Miles Lane	43
Nazareth	44
Old Winchester	45
Philippi	46
Richmond	47
St. Agnes	424
St. Ann's	48
St. James	49
St. Magnus	50
St. Peter	51
St. Saviour	52

	NO.
St. Stephen	53
Sawley	54
Solomon	55
Sympathy	425
Tallis	56
Tiverton	57
Warwick	58
Westminster	59

8.6.8.6., with Refrain.

Anniversary	60
Children's Jubilee	63
Glory	61
Glory	62
Heaven	64
O Paradise	67
O Paradise	68
Return, O wanderer	72
St. Winifred	69
Sweet Sabbath School	71

8.6.8.6.8.6.

Spohr	65

8.6.8.6.8.8.

Redemption	66

8.6.8.6. D.

Audite Audientes me	73
Castle Rising	426
Ellacombe	74
Land of Rest	75
Noël	76
Palestine	77
Prospect	78
St. Matthew	79
Spes Celestis	80
There is a green	81

8.6. 12 lines.

Auld Lang Syne	70
Christmas Bells	82

Long Metres.

8.8.8.8.

Alsace	427
Alstone	428
Angelus	83
Beethoven	84
Boston	85
Canonbury	86
Doversdale	87
Eden	88
Eisenach	89
Ernan	90
Evening Hymn	91
Gibraltar	92
Holley	93
Honiton	94
Hursley	95
Luther's Chant	96
Mainzer	97

	NO.
Melcombe	98
Montgomery	99
Morning Hymn	100
Neapolis	101
Old 100th	102
Ombersley	103
Rockingham	104
Samson	105
Simeon	106
Wandsworth	107
Warrington	108
Whitburn	109
Winchester	110
Woolstanton	111

8.8.8.8.D. or with Ref'n.

Anniversary Song	112
Creation	113
O happy day	116
Stand up for Jesus	115
Sweet hour of prayer	114

4.10.10.10.4.

Bluntisham	117

5.5.5.3.5.5.5.4. with Refrain.

Sound the battle cry	118

5.5.5.11.

Winchcombe	119

5.5.11. D.

Harwich	120

5.5.5.11. D.

Hosanna	121

5.5 5.6.6.8.

O sing to the Lord	123

5.6.5.6. D.

Emmeline	124

5.6.6.4.

St. Hilda	122

5.6.6.5.9.

Harvest	125

6.4.6.4.

Nain	126

6.4. 12 lines.

Valentia	127

6.4.6.4.6.6.6.4.

Beulah	129
Nearer to Thee	130
Saviour, Thy dying	128

6.4.6.4.6.7.6.4.

Indiana	131

6.4.6.4.10.10.

Budleigh	132

5.5.6.5.

Derby	133

	NO.
Evensong	134
North Coates	135
St. Clothilde	136
St. Jude	137
St. Lambert	138

6.5.6.5. D.

Franconia	139
If I come to Jesus	140
Jesus is our Shepherd	141
Lyndhurst	431
Mountmellick	432
Pilgrim Song	433
St. Cephas	142
St. Mary Magdalene	143
Vespers	144
Woodbrook	434

6.5.6.5. 12 lines.

Coppet	146
Deva	435
Fleury	145
Haydn	147
Hermas	148
Parkholme	438
Ruth	150
St. Gertrude	149
Strike for Vict'ry	152
Sumus Tibi	436

6.5.6.5.7.7.6 5.

Crosby	151

6.5.6.4. with Refrain.

Christ arose	153

6.6.4.6.6.6.4.

Blandford	154
Brockley	155
Moscow	156
Nat'nal Anthem	157
Newhaven	158
Olivet	159

6.4.6.4.6.6.6.4. with Refrain.

Christine	160

6.6.6.6.

Amaranth	161
Dolomite Chant	429
Mount St. Bernard	162
St. Cecilia	163

6.6.6.6.6.6.

Danbury	164
Oasis	165

6.6.6.6. D.

Agatha	166
Bury St. Edmunds	167

6.6.6.6. D. with Ref'n.

Come to the Saviour	168
Invitation	439

NO.

6.6.6.6.8.8.
Children's Voices ... 170
Darwells 171
Echo Song 172
Exeter 173
Leslie... 442
Safe Home 174
St. John 175
Samuel 176
6.6.8.4.
Verbum Pacis... ... 177
6.6.8.4. D.
Laudamus 178
6.6.8.6.10.12.
Inglewhite 169
7.5.7.5.
Ariel 180
7.5.7.5. D.
Morden 182
7.5.7.5. D. with Refrain.
Intercession 179
7.5.7.5.4.7.4.5. with Refrain.
The golden rule ... 184
7.5.7.5.7.7.
Gawthorpe 181
Silksworth 443
7.5.7.5.7.7.7.5.
At the Cross there's 183
7.6.5.5.5.6.4.6. and Refrain.
One more day's work 186
One more day's work 187
7.6.7.5. D.
Work for the night 185
7.6.7.6.
Autumn 188
Barton 189
Sacrifice 190
St. Alphege 191
St. Philip... 192
7.6.7.6.6.6.7.6.
Jesus keep me near 193
7.6.7.6.7.6.7.3.
Pilgrimage 194
7.6.7.6. D.
Alpha 444
Angel's Story 195
Aurelia 196
Carbrooke 445
Chenies 446
Come unto Me ... 197
Day of rest 198
Dedham 199
Dunkirk 200
Ewing 202
Fairford 448
Greenland 203
Harlington 201
Heber 204
Lux Mundi 449
Lymington 205
Mendelssohn 450
Missionary 206
Mossleigh... 207
Munich 208
New York 209

NO.

Rutherford 451
St. George's Bolton 210
St. Theodulph... ... 211
Savoy Chapel 452
Schubert 212
Shiloh (Endsleigh)... 213
The Golden Chain... 447
Tours... 456
7.6.7.6. D. with Refrain.
Benignus 214
God bless the Prince
of Wales 466
How many sheep are 223
I love the name ... 217
I love to tell 215
Newark 222
Safe in the arms ... 219
Tell me the old, old 218
There is a holy City 453
We plough the fields 220
7.6.7.6.7.6.8.6.
Sing with a tuneful 224
7.6.7.6.7.7.7.6.
Follow Me 221
7.6.7.6.8.8.
St. Anatolius 225
7.6.8.6.
St. Alphege 216
7.6.8.6.7.6.8.6.
Bellevue 226
Civitas Dei 457
7.6.8.6.8.6.8.6.
Beneath the Cross ... 229
St. Christopher ... 458
Trevu 227
Wiclif 228
7.7.6. and Refrain.
Joyful 230
7.7.7.
Lacrymæ 231
7.7.7.3.
Vigilate 232
7.7.7.5.
Cape Town 233
Irene 430
Trinitas 437
Wanswell... 234
7.7.7.7.
Chester 235
Dijon... 236
Ellingham 237
German Hymn ... 238
Hart's 239
Innocents... 240
Kiel 241
Nottingham 242
Percy... 243
Pulchra 244
Redhead 245
Solicitude... 246
Theodora 247
University College... 248
7.7.7.7. with Refrain.
Children of Jerus'l'm 249
Easter Hymn 250
Jesus loves me ... 252

NO.

7.7.7.7.7.
Haverstock 251
7.7.7.7.7.7.
Ashburton 454
Cassel 253
Dix 254
Eglon... 256
Morning Star 257
Nassau 255
Requiem 258
Spain... 259
Wells... 260
7.7.7.7. D.
Benevento 261
Christmas Hymn ... 263
Easter Hymn 250
Hollingside 262
Honidon 265
Iona 264
St. Agnes... 459
St.George's,Windsor 266
Syria 267
7s. 10 lines.
Nocturne 269
7.7.7.7.8.5.8.5.
Shadows 270
7.7.8.7.8.7.
Knocking 271
7.7.8.8.7.7.
I am Jesus' little fri'nd 272
Tromso 273
7.8.7.6.9.9.9.6. and Refrain.
Beautiful home ... 268
8.3.8.3.8.8.8.3.
Come, let us all unite 274
Tabor... 276
8.4.8.4.8.8.8.4.
Jesus, little children 277
8.5.8.3.
Brookfield 275
Bullinger 278
Consolator 279
Rothbury 440
Stephanos... 280
8.5.8.5.8.4.3.
Angel Voices 281
8.5.8.5. and Refrain.
Pass me not 282
8.6.6.8.6.6.
Nativity 284
8.6.7.6.7.6.7.6.
Newport 283
8.6.8.4.
Wreford 286
8.6.8.5.8.8.8.5.
The sweetest name... 287
8.6.8.5. with Refrain.
When He cometh ... 285
8.7.8.4.
Star of Peace 288
8.7.8.7.
Baun 289
Day by Day 290
Galilee 455
Lausanne 291
Lucerne 292

NO.

Mariners 293
St. Helen 294
St. Mabyn 295
Sardis 296
Sefton 297
Sharon 298
8.7.8.7.3.
Even me 299
8.7.8.7. with Refrain.
Brightly beams our 300
Shall we gather ... 302
Shall we meet 301
8.7.8.7.8.7.
Benedicite 303
Braylesford 304
Calvary 305
Dismissal 306
Mannheim 307
Regent Square ... 308
Rousseau 309
St. Werburgh 310
Triumph 311
8.7.8.7.7.7.
Evensong 312
Gounod 313
8.7.8.7. D.
Austria 314
Angelic Host 315
Benediction 316
Bethany 317
Chichester 318
Florence 319
Vesper 320
What a friend 321
8.7.8.7.8.8.4.8.
Our Sabbath Song ... 322
8.7.8.7. D. with Refrain.
Canaan 324
Beacon 325
8.7.8.7.8.8.8.7.
Whither, Pilgrims ... 326
8.7.8.9. D. with Refrain.
Listen! the Master 327
8.8.6.8.8.6.
Hereford 323
Praise 328
8.8.8.4.
Handford 329
Resignation 330
Selattyn 331
Shoreham 332
8.8.8.6.
Agnus Dei 333
Elmhurst 441
Just as I am 334
Humility 335
8.8.8.8. with Refrain.
Celeste 336
8.8.8.8.8.8.
Monmouth 339
Pater Omnium ... 460
St. Matthias 337
Stella 338
8.8.6.5.8. and Refrain.
There's a beautiful 341
8.9.9.8. and Refrain.
O think of the home 342

NO.

9.7.9.7.9.9.
Compassion 343
9.8.9.8.8.8.
Friburg 340
9.8.9.8. D.
A crowd fills the ... 344
Clarion 345
9.9.9.9.7.7. and Refrain.
Sowing the seed ... 347
9.10.9.9.10.10.6.
The better land ... 346
10.8.10.8. and Refrain.
Thou didst leave ... 349
Veni Domine Jesu ... 461
10.8.10.8. D. and Refrain.
March of life 348
10.8.11.8. with Refrain.
The Master is come 350
10.9.10.9. and Refrain.
Lead me to Jesus ... 353
10.9.10.9.10.8.10.8.
Seraphim 352
10.10.4.6.
Yet there is room ... 351
10.10.10.10.
Ellers 354
Eventide 355
Pax Dei 356
St. Agnes 357
Toulon 358
10.10.10.10. and Refrain.
The good old way ... 361
10.10.10.10.4.
Aylesbury 359
It passeth knowledge 462
Patmos 360
10.10.10.10.10.10.
Yorkshire 362
Tenterden 363
10.10.10.10. D.
Joyfully 365
10.10.11.11.
Hanover 364
Houghton 366
St. Patrick 367
10s. & 11s. 8 lines, irregular.
Endsleigh 369
Hosanna we sing ... 465
10.11.11.11.12.11.10.11.
Sound the loud ... 370
10.13.10.9. with Refrain.
On to the conflict ... 368
11.7.11.7. with Refrain.
Beautiful stream ... 373
Beautiful stream ... 463
11.8.11.8.
How sweet is the ... 371
Belfield 372
11.8.11.9.11.9.11.9.
Athens 376
11 9.11.9. with Refrain.
Ring the bells 374
11.10.11.10.
Epiphany Hymn ... 377
Marlborough 378
11.9.12.9.
A crown for the ... 375

NO.

11.10.11.10.9.11.
Hark, hark my soul 380
Pilgrims 381
11.11.
Salome 379
11.11. with Refrain.
Rejoice and be glad 382
11.11.11.7. D.
We are marching on 383
11.11.11.11.
Foundation 387
Oldenburg 384
Rest 385
St. Luke 386
11.11.11.11. with Refrain.
Columbia 395
Dear Sav'r, we gather 388
Erastus 394
Home, sweet home ... 389
I have a Saviour ... 390
Love one another ... 392
O Christian, awake 391
So near to the 393
11.11.11.11.11.11.
St. Faith 396
11.12.12.10.
Nicæa 397
12.7.12.7. with Refrain.
In the highways ... 398
12.8.11.8. with Refrain.
Heaven, sweet heaven 464
There's a beautiful 399
12.9.11.9.
There is life 400
There is life 401
13.11.13.12.
Ems 402
13.13.8.8.10.
Salem 403

Double Chants.

Alcock 407
Aldrich 408
Boyce 409
Crotch 410
Dupuis 411
Handel 412
Henley 413
Langdon 414
Mornington 415
Robinson 416

Metrical Chants.

Reynolds 417
Selattyn 331
Troyte (No. 1) 418
Troyte (No. 2) 404

I will arise 420
Musical Dream ... 419
Sanctus 405
Springtime 406
Te Deum Laudamus 422
Vital Spark 421

ALPHABETICAL INDEX OF HYMNS.

HYMN		TUNE
34	A crowd fills the court of the	... 344
326	A thought is but a little thing	41, 47
241	A year again has passed away	... 60
177	Abide with me !	... 355, 418
393	Above the clear blue sky, ...	... 170
437	Accepting, Lord, Thy gracious..	... 441
23	All hail the power of Jesus' name	43
25	All my heart this night rejoices	284
	All thanks be to God	... 121
10	All things (except first verse)	... 188
7	All things praise Thee, Lord	... 257
	All ye that pass-by	...120
12	Almighty God, Thy piercing eye	56
258	Always with us, always with	295, 297
373	And now another day is gone	... 58
483	And shall we dwell together	... 191
449	Angel voices ever singing ...	... 281
195	Another Sabbath ended ...	... 196
186	Another six days' work is done	100
182	Another year is dawning ...	... 192
392	Around the throne of God ...	61, 62
90	Art thou weary, art thou ...	279, 280
487	As the bird in meadow fair	... 459
30	As with gladness men of old	... 254
173	At even, ere the sun was set	... 83
45	At the name of Jesus	... 139
249	At Thy feet, our God and Father	320
431	Awake, for the trumpet is...	... 345
235	Baptized into Thy name most holy	340
235	Beautiful home of the blest	... 268
224	Beneath the cross of Jesus...	229, 458
142	Beyond the dark river a land I	389
422	Blessed Jesus, life is fair ...	... 243
29	Brightest and best of the sons of	377
211	Brightly beams our Father's	... 300
301	Brightly gleams our banner	... 147
379	By cool Siloam's shady rill...	28, 31
391	Can I, a little child	... 173
309	Captain and Saviour of Thine	24, 46
362	Childhood's years are passing o'er	293
450	Children above are singing	189, 192
243	Children join to praise the Saviour	294
342	Children of Jerusalem... ...	... 249
39	Christ the Lord is risen to-day...	250
266	Christ was teaching all the	241, 244
	Christian, seek not yet repose ...	232
31	Christians, awake, salute the	... 362
163	Come at the morning hour...	... 13
335	Come, children, let us go ...	4, 16
213	Come, Christian children, come	27
205	Come, Christian youths and	... 205
345	Come, happy children, come and	50
246	Come, Holy Ghost, in love...	156, 159
66	Come, Holy Ghost, our	27, 53, 415
68	Come, Holy Ghost, the Comforter	33
279	Come, labour on	... 117
202	Come, let us all unite and sing...	274
318	Come, let us join the hosts above	27, 31
337	Come, let us praise the Prince	45, 52
208	Come, let us sing of Jesus ...	... 203
212	Come, praise your Lord ...	205, 211
	Do. vrs. 1, 4.. 209; v. 2...211, v. 3...196	

HYMN		TUNE
47	Come, Thou Fount of every	... 316
351	Come to Jesus, little one ...	... 180
95	Come to the Saviour now ...	168, 439
434	Come unto Me, the Saviour	73, 426
94	Come unto Me, ye weary ...	... 197
180	Come, ye thankful people, come	266
43	Crown Him with many crowns	20
207	Day by day we magnify Thee ...	290
414	Dear Jesus, ever at my side	26, 29
260	Dear Lord and Master mine	... 5, 9
348	Dear Saviour, we gather our	... 388
	Depth of mercy, can there be	... 265
293	Dismiss me not Thy service, Lord	65
272	Do not I love Thee, O my Lord	42, 424
126	Draw nearer, my Saviour ...	... 386
178	Earth below is teeming ...	... 150
	Eternal Power, whose high abode	86
75	Ever-blessed Trinity ...	... 234, 437
330	Every little step I take ...	... 247
398	Every morning the red sun	181, 443
200	Fair waved the golden corn	... 4
417	Father, by Thy love and power	269
181	Father, here we dedicate ...	... 182
316	Father, lead me day by day	... 247
22	Father, let Thy benediction	... 303
154	Father of heaven, bless ...	155, 156
375	Father, while the shadows fall...	270
285	Fearless, calm, and strong in love	233
432	Follow Me, the Master saith	... 221
	For all Thy love and goodness...	406
	For all Thy saints who from	... 404
134	For ever with the Lord ...	... 21
62	For the beauty of the earth	... 255
196	For Thy mercy and Thy grace...	248
298	Forward be our watchword	149, 438
161	From all that dwell below...	102, 110
	From every stormy wind that ...	111
157	From Greenland's icy ...	... 203, 204
158	From the eastern mountains	... 144
242	From year to year in love we meet	92
336	Gentle Jesus, full of grace...	... 259
346	Gentle Jesus, meek and mild	... 239
70	Glory be to God the Father	... 311
401	Glory, glory, to God in the	... 352
63	Glory to God on high	... 156
176	Glory to Thee, my God, this night	91
74	Glory to the Father give ...	... 246
290	Go, labour on, spend and be spent	84
129	Go when the morning shineth	199, 444
289	Go work for God and do not say	39, 54
72	God Almighty, in Thy temple...	310
489	God bless our dear old England	466
245	God bless our native land ...	... 157
244	God bless our Sunday School	154, 156
332	God intrusts to all	... 124
407	God is in heaven. Can He hear?	56
18	God is love, His mercy ...	298, 292
321	God loves the little sparrows	... 212
16	God might have made the earth	44
402	God of glory, God of grace	... 264

HYMN	TUNE
408 God of mercy and of love	264
383 God of mercy, throned on high	238
240 God of the heaven and earth ...	161
331 God sets a still small voice ...	162
333 God, who made the earth	122
42 Golden harps are sounding ...	148
377 Good night, good night, the day	24
440 Gracious Saviour, holy ... 306, 307
67 Gracious Spirit, dwell with 254, 255
20 Great God, and wilt Thou... ...	97
84 Great God, with wonder and 55, 59
21 Guide me, O Thou great	309
475 Hail, sweetest, dearest	70
197 Hail the children's festal day ...	266
38 Hail the day that sees Him rise	248
159 Hail to the Lord's anointed ...	209
5 Hallelujah ! praise the Lord ...	251
367 Happy the child whose youngest	34
354 Hark, a still small voice	253
92 Hark ! a thrilling voice is	296
145 Hark ! hark ! my soul, angelic 380, 381
26 Hark, the glad sound ! the Saviour	52
27 Hark, the herald angels sing ...	263
156 Hark, the voice of Jesus crying	314
350 Hark ! 'tis the Saviour calls 7, 17
28 Hark ! 'tis the song of heaven 10, 17
411 Hark ! what mean those holy ...	315
385 Heavenly Father, we draw 304, 307
378 Here, we suffer grief and pain ...	230
363 Holy Bible, book Divine ... 235, 239
73 Holy Father, hear my cry	245
71 Holy, Holy, Holy, Lord God ...	397
Holy ! Holy ! Holy ! (Sanctus) ...	405
64 Holy Spirit ! hear us	138
65 Holy Spirit, Truth divine ... 239, 243
344 Hosanna be the children's song	63
204 Hosanna ! raise the pealing hymn	57
214 Hosanna we sing, like the ... 369, 465
284 How blessed from the bonds of 75, 77
13 How dearly God must love 188, 192
How firm a foundation, ye 387, 402
312 How glorious is our heavenly ...	49
78 How holy the Bible ! how 371, 372
426 How kind is the Saviour ... 386, 387
469 How many sheep are straying ..	223
83 How shall the young secure 25, 48
308 How softly on the western hills	36
188 How sweet is the Sabbath... ...	394
48 How sweet the name of Jesus ...	51
477 Hush ! blessed are the dead ...	429
89 Hushed was the evening hymn...	176
358 I am Jesus' little friend	272
357 I am Jesus' little lamb	273
419 I am trusting Thee, Lord Jesus	440
359 I belong to Jesus	143
448 I could not do without Thee ...	210
479 I dream'd, and lo, 't was	419
111 I give my heart to Thee	19
445 I have a Saviour	390
282 I have a work, O Lord 1, 15
444 I hear a sweet voice ringing clear 276
57 I heard the voice of Jesus say ...	73
474 I hear thee speak of a better land	346
451 I know there's a crown	375
56 I lay my sins on Jesus	206
I lift my heart to Thee	132
421 I love my precious Saviour 446, 447
52 I love the name of Jesus	217
121 I love Thy kingdom, Lord... ...	1
53 I love to hear the story ... 195, 222
420 I love to sing of that great power	40
120 I love to tell the story... ... 214, 215
33 I love to think, though I am ...	40
127 I need Thee, precious Jesus ...	210
485 I often say my prayers	11
438 I ought to love my Saviour 195, 450
11 I sing the Almighty power of God	53
347 I think when I read that sweet ...	376
353 I want to be like Jesus	216
I was a wandering sheep ... 22, 23
490 I will arise	420
110 I would a youthful pilgrim be ...	85
356 If I come to Jesus 140, 432
380 If Jesus Christ was sent ... 13, 15
I'll praise my Maker	339
352 I'm a little pilgrim 137, 433
109 In full and glad surrender... ...	190
467 In our work, and in our play ...	240
220 In Shiloh, where Thine ark 39, 47
370 In the highways and hedges ...	398
476 In the march of life	348
325 In the name of Jesus 146, 148
323 In the wintry heaven	142
441 Is there one heart, dear Saviour	425
24 It came upon the midnight ...	76
436 It is a thing most wonderful 89, 427
307 It is not death to die	9
119 It passeth knowledge ... 359, 360, 462
151 Jerusalem the golden	202
162 Jesus, blessed Saviour... ... 145, 435
277 Jesus calls us o'er the tumult ...	297
340 Jesus Christ, my Lord and ...	317
322 Jesus, Friend of little 275, 278
415 Jesus, great Redeemer	143
343 Jesus, high in glory	133
50 Jesus, I love Thy charming name	24
263 Jesus, in Thy blest name ... 14, 16
59 Jesus is our Pilot 146, 147
423 Jesus is our Shepherd	141
465 Jesus, keep me near the Cross ...	193
442 Jesus little children blesses ...	277
191 Jesus, Lord of Sabbath rest ...	241
58 Jesus ! lover of my soul	262
341 Jesus loves me ! this I know ...	252
292 Jesus, Master, whom I serve ...	253
453 Jesus, meek and lowly	133
261 Jesus, Saviour, Brother, Lord ...	242
61 Jesus shall reign where'er	103
439 Jesus, tender Saviour...	434
376 Jesus, tender Shepherd, hear 297, 298
264 Jesus, the Friend of Friendless	47
267 Jesus, the sinners' friend	4, 5
49 Jesus, the very thought of Thee	26
Jesus to Thy table led...	231
413 Jesus, we come to Thee	21
368 Jesus, we love to meet	167
339 Jesus, when a little child ... 253, 259
466 Jesus, when He left the sky ...	430
338 Jesus, who lived above the sky	95
144 Joyfully, joyfully, onward we ...	365
115 Just as I am, without one ... 333, 334
328 Kind words can never die	160
99 Knocking, knocking, who is there	271
80 Lamp of our feet, whereby 32, 414
233 Lead me to Jesus...	353
257 Lead us, heavenly Father, lead	304

HYMN		TUNE	HYMN		TUNE
203	Let all assembled here	17	256	O Lord, revive Thy work	2,18
314	Let children proclaim	364	405	O Lord, while life and hope are	47
77	Let everlasting glories crown	99		O Master, at Thy feet	169
313	Let us sing with one accord	237	122	O my Saviour, hear me	151
3	Let us with a gladsome mind	240	148	O Paradise ! O Paradise	67, 68
472	Life is real, life is earnest	455	416	O Saviour, precious Saviour	445
280	Listen, the Master beseecheth	327	54	O sing to the Lord	123
329	Little drops of water	136	364	O that I like Timothy	253, 259
399	Little travellers Zionward	267	201	O Thou, whose hand hath brought	201
105	Lo ! a loving friend is waiting	278	165	O timely happy, timely wise	104
36	Lo ! at noon 'tis sudden night	258	454	O walk with Jesus	85
486	Lo ! from the eastern hills, the	48	8	O worship the King, all	366, 367
404	Lord, from this time we cry	337, 460	463	O'er the wide and restless ocean	325
248	Lord, from whom all blessings	261	276	Oft when of God we ask	442
275	Lord, give me light to do Thy	54	259	Oh, bless the Lord and praise	171
193	Lord, how delightful 'tis to see	88	98	Oh ! come in life's gay morning	190
114	Lord, I hear of showers of blessing	299	101	Oh! do not let the word depart	90
320	Lord, I read of tender mercy	275	143	Oh ! have you not heard of a	373, 463
	Lord, I was blind, I could not see	87	291	Oh ! it is hard to work for God	41
317	Lord, I would own Thy tender	34, 40	315	Oh ! Lord, our strength and	201
155	Lord of the living harvest	211	147	Oh ! think of the home over there	342
252	Lord, speak to me, that I may	93	55	Oh ! what has Jesus done for me	324
381	Lord, teach a little child to	40, 54	461	On to the conflict	368
406	Lord, Thy children guide and	454	216	On toward Zion, on	167
273	Lord, we bring our work to	239, 244	198	Once more with joyous	211, 213
247	Lord, we meet to pray and	261, 267	306	One by one the saints are	301, 317
102	Lost one ! wandering on in	288	295	One more day's work for	186, 187
430	Low in the grave He lay	153	44	One there is above all others	313
274	Make use of me, my God	11, 17	455	Onward, Christian, through the	290
135	Mansions are prepared above	235, 241	69	Our blest Redeemer ere He	286
456	March onward, march onward	395	169	Our day of praise is done	6, 15
46	Mighty God, while angels	314, 318	424	Our loving Redeemer, we trust	396
32	My dear Redeemer and my Lord	101	113	Pass me not, O gracious Saviour	282
125	My faith looks up to Thee	159	400	Praise God, from whom all	102
106	My God, accept my heart	46	1	Praise, my soul, the King of	308
166	My God, is any hour so	329, 331	4	Praise the Lord, ye	294, 1st part 320
132	My God, my Father	330, 332, 417	253	Reign in my heart, great God	177
371	My God, who makes the sun	30, 50	206	Rejoice and be glad, the Redeemer	382
268	My gracious God, I own Thy right	98		Return, O wanderer, return	72
	My Jesus, as Thou wilt	166	255	Revive Thy work, O Lord	10
457	Mourner, wheresoe'er thou art	183	324	Ring, ring the bells, the joyful	82
9	My soul, repeat His praise	16	199	Ring the bells of heaven	374
124	Nearer, my God, to Thee	129, 130	183	Rise, heart ! thy Lord arose	3, 14
334	Never lose the golden rule	184	116	Rock of Ages, cleft for me	260
	Not all the blood of beasts	8	96	Room for the wanderer, room	4, 13
112	Now in my early days	1, 16		Safe home, safe home in port	174
366	Now that my journey's just	25, 32	150	Safe in the arms of Jesus	219
167	Now the day is over	134, 431	238	Sailing on the ocean	147
281	Now, the sowing and the	292, 298		Saved ourselves by Jesus' blood	256
462	O Christian, awake	391	170	Saviour, abide with us	6
187	O day of rest and gladness	213	194	Saviour, again to Thy dear	354, 356
40	O for a shout of sacred joy	38	360	Saviour, bless a little child	236
	O for the peace that floweth	378	51	Saviour, blessed Saviour	145
19	O God of Bethel, by whose hand	25	175	Saviour, breathe an evening	291, 319
349	O God, our offerings we present	29	386	Saviour, like a Shepherd lead us	307
299	O happy band of pilgrims	189	384	Saviour, round Thy footstool	306
117	O happy day that fix'd my	94, 116	459	Saviour, teach me day by day	241
139	O happy land ! O happy land !	77	412	Saviour, Thy dying love	128
311	O heaven, sweet heaven	385	131	Saviour, while my heart is tender	298
361	O Jesus, behold	119	294	Saviour, who Thy flock art	295
262	O Jesus, ever present	190, 196	232	Shall hymns of grateful love	172
271	O Jesus, I have promised	198	433	Shall Jesus bid the children come	30
128	O Jesus, meek and lowly	208	254	Shall this life of mine be wasted	291
107	O Jesus, Saviour, we are young	46, 54	146	Shall we gather at the river	302
108	O Jesus, Thou art standing	207	236	Shall we meet beyond the river	301
418	O joy to see Thee, Jesus	188	464	Shepherd dear, and fair, and holy	309
123	O Lamb of God, most lowly	191	390	Shepherd of tender youth	156, 158
251	O Lord of Glory, be my light	105	425	Sing a hymn to Jesus	145

HYMN		TUNE
2	Sing to the Lord a joyful song...	106
319	Sing to the Lord the children's	31
403	Sing with a tuneful spirit	224
481	So near to the kingdom	393
192	Softly fades the twilight ray ...	236
300	Soldiers of Christ, arise	7
6	Songs of praise the angels ...	237, 240
382	Soon as my youthful lips can ...	26
190	Soon shall set the Sabbath sun...	244
458	Sound the battle cry	118
226	Sound the loud timbrel o'er ...	370
278	Sow in the morn thy seed	11
228	Sowing the seed in the morning	347
234	Speak gently, it is better far	77, 78
283	Spirit of holiness descend ...	51, 53
225	Stand up for Jesus, Christian ...	115
	Stand up, my soul	107
302	Stand up! stand up for Jesus 200,	448
410	Star of eternal day	127
460	Strike, O strike for victory ...	152
488	Summer suns are glowing	150
172	Sun of my soul, Thou Saviour 95,	109
133	Sweet hour of prayer, sweet ...	114
369	Sweet Sabbath school, more dear	71
174	Sweet Saviour, bless us ere	337, 338
37	Sweet spices they brought on ...	379
	Sweet the moments, rich in ...	289
478	Sweetly dawns the Sabbath ...	322
164	Sweetly the holy hymn ...	5, 423
269	Take my life, and let it be... ...	235
305	Teach me to live! 'tis easier far	358
	Te Deum Laudamus	422
60	Tell me the old, old story	218
153	Ten thousand times ten ...	226, 457
428	Ten thousand times ten thousand	66
79	The Bible! the Bible! more ...	384
447	The central joy in glory land ...	27
372	The darkness now is over	188
	The day is gently sinking	363
171	The day is past and over	225
168	The day was done, beside the ...	354
185	The dawn of God's dear Sabbath	451
	The festal morn, my God, is come	328
387	The fields are all white	125
286	The Galilean fishers toil	79
	The God of Abraham praise ...	178
41	The golden gates are lifted up ...	55
409	The hours of day are over	452
	The light of Sabbath eve	15
287	The livelong night we've toiled 25,	56
91	The Master is come, and calleth	350
85	The praises of my tongue	3
149	The roseate hues of early dawn 75,	426
	The Sabbath day has reached ...	335
87	The Saviour calls, let every ear	48
480	The shadows of the evening hours	24
	The spacious firmament on high	113
303	The Son of God goes forth to war	74
	The strain upraise	404
446	The sweetest name in heaven ...	287
484	The world looks very beautiful...	194
395	There is a better world	276
452	There is a clime	69
394	There is a glorious world of	53, 64
35	There is a green hill far away	35, 81
237	There is a happy land...	131
136	There is a heaven of perfect peace	29
473	There is a holy city	453
152	There is a land of pure delight...	78
118	There is a name I love to hear ...	37
388	There is a path that leads to God	32
227	There is a precious day '	15
104	There is life for a look... ...	400, 401
137	There is no night in heaven ...	4
	There were ninety-and-nine ...	343
396	There's a beautiful land on high	341
140	There's a beautiful land where 399,	464
355	There's a friend for little children	283
15	There's not a tint	28
427	This is my commandment	392
184	This is the day of light	12
189	This is the day the Lord hath ...	45
	Thou art gone up on high	18
310	Thou art gone to the grave, but...	402
231	Thou didst leave Thy throne 349,	461
160	Thou, whose Almighty word ...	158
374	Through the day Thy love has...	312
270	Thy life was given for me ... 164,	165
81	Thy word is like a garden ...	29, 34
471	Time is earnest, passing by ...	238
304	'Tis but a veil that hangs between	39
93	To-day the Saviour calls	126
97	To-day Thy mercy calls ...	210, 449
179	To praise the ever bounteous	45, 57
76	To the name of God on high ...	246
250	To whom but unto Thee	1, 17
	Triumphant, Lord, Thy goodness	108
	Vital Spark	421
130	Was there ever kindest ...	293, 298
296	Watch and pray, fast fades ...	418
	Weary of earth, and laden with	357
468	We are but little children weak	428
223	We are going forth with our staff	361
222	We are marching on with shield	383
210	We bring no glittering ...	205, 209
217	We love the good old Bible	211, 213
265	We love the place, O God	163
470	We plough the fields	220
209	We sing a loving Jesus ...	195, 206
215	We sing our song of Jubilee ...	112
138	We speak of the realms of the ...	336
86	We won't give up the Bible	74, 228
218	We won't give up the Sabbath 74,	227
397	We're marching to the promised	64
229	What can I give to Jesus	216
230	What a Friend we have in Jesus	321
141	When He cometh, when He ...	285
443	When, His salvation bringing 200,	456
82	When Israel through the desert	89
88	When little Samuel woke	175
482	When mothers of Salem	403
14	When o'er the earth is breaking	135
435	When the day of life is dawning	277
	When the weary seeking rest ...	179
	When Thou, my righteous judge	323
365	When to the House of God we go	109
429	While shepherds watched	80
221	Whither, pilgrims, are you going	326
219	Who is on the Lord's side ... 146,	436
327	Words are things of little cost 253,	259
288	Work, for the night is coming ...	185
100	Ye hearts with youthful vigour 30,	58
297	Ye servants of the Lord	14
17	Yes, God is good: in earth and	96
239	Yes, we part, but not for ever ...	305
103	Yet there is room	351
389	Young children once to Jesus	36, 47

THE TREASURY,

A

Companion Tune Book

TO

"PSALMS AND HYMNS FOR SCHOOL AND HOME.

1 AUGUSTINE. S.M. J. S. BACH.

I love Thy king-dom, Lord, The house of Thine a-bode;

The Church our blest Re-deem-er saved With His own pre-cious blood.

2 BRIGHTON. S.M. DR. MASON.

"O Lord, re-vive Thy work!" Bid showers of grace des-cend;

To long-ing hearts re-veal Thy love, And save us to the end.

3 CAMBRIDGE.   S.M.   REV. R. HARRISON.

The prais - es of my tongue I of - fer to my Lord,

That I was taught, and learned so young To read His ho - ly word.

4 CARLISLE.*   S.M.   LOCKHART.

There is no night in heaven! In that blest world a - bove

Work nev - er can bring wea - ri - ness, For work it - self is love.

5 FRANCONIA.   S.M.   German.

Sweet - ly the ho - ly hymn Breaks on the morn - ing air;

Be - fore the world with smoke is dim We meet to of - fer prayer

6 **LANGTON.**   S.M.   Adapted by C. STREATFIELD.

Sa . viour, a - bide with us; The day is now far gone;

We would ob - tain a bless - ing thus, By com-ing to Thy throne.

7 **LOUDON.** *   S.M.   OLMSTEAD.   From " Congregational Church Music."

Sol - diers of Christ, a - rise, And put your ar - mour on;

Strong in the strength which God sup - plies Thro' His e - ter - nal Son.

8 **MOUNT EPHRAIM.**   S.M.   MILGROVE.

Not all the blood of beasts, On Jew - ish al - tars slain,

Could give the guil - ty con - science peace, Or wash a - way the stain.

3.

9 ST. AUSTIN.   S.M.   REV. AUSTIN E. LORD.

It is not death to die, To leave this wea - ry road,

And 'midst the bro - ther - hood on high, To be at home with God.

10 ST. GEORGE.   S.M.   DR. GAUNTLETT.

Re - vive Thy work, O Lord, Thy migh - ty arm make bare;

Speak with the voice that wakes the dead, And make Thy peo - ple hear.

11 ST. MICHAEL. *   S.M.   GUILLAUME FRANC, 1543.

Sow in the morn thy seed, At eve hold not thine hand:

To doubt and fear give thou no heed, Broad - cast it o'er the land.

12 SERENITY. S.M. C. BRYAN.

This is the day of light: Let there be light to-day;

O day-spring rise up-on our night, And chase its gloom a-way.

13 SHIRLAND. S.M. JOHN STANLEY.

Come at the morn-ing hour, Come, let us kneel and pray;

Prayer is the Chris-tian pil-grim's staff To walk with God all day.

14 SILCHESTER. S.M. REV. DR. MALAN.

Ye ser-vants of the Lord, Each in his of-fice wait,

Ob-ser-vant of His heaven-ly word, And watch-ful at His gate.

15 TAMERTON.   S.M.   From "Congregational Church Music."

The light of Sab - bath eve Is fad - ing fast a - way;

What pleas - ing re - cord will it leave To crown the clos - ing day?

16 TYTHERTON.   S.M.   Rev. L. R. West.

My soul, re - peat His praise Whose mer - cies are so great,

Whose an - ger is so slow to rise, So rea - dy to a - bate.

17 TUAM. *   S.M.   W. Mason.

Let all as - sem - bled here, On this re - turn - ing day,

Re - view the mer - cies of the year, And grate - ful ho - mage pay.

18 ASCENSION.

S.M. Dble.

DR. GAUNTLETT

Voices in UNISON.

HARMONY.

Thou art gone up on high To man-sions in the skies; And round Thy throne un-

-ceas-ing-ly The songs of praise a-rise. But we are lin-g'ring here, With

cres.

sin and care op-pressed, Lord, send Thy promised Comfort-er, And lead us to our rest.

19 ASSURANCE.

S.M. Dble.

"Lausanne Psalter."

I give my heart to Thee, O Je-sus, most de-sired! And heart for heart the

gift shall be, For Thou my soul hast fired; Thou hearts a-lone wouldst move, Thou

on-ly hearts dost love; I would love Thee as Thou lov'st me, O Je-sus, most de-sired!

20 DIADEMATA. S.M., Dble. Sir George J. Elvey, Mus.Doc. From "Hymns Ancient and Modern," by per.

Crown Him with ma - ny crowns, The Lamb up - on His throne ; Hark ! how the heaven-ly

an-them drowns All mu - sic but its own : A - wake, my soul, and sing Of

Him who died for thee, And hail Him as thy cho-sen King Thro' all e - ter - ni - ty.

21 NEARER HOME. S.M. Dble., with Chorus. J. B. Woodbury.

"For ev - er with the Lord !" A-men, so let it be ; Life from the dead is in that word, 'Tis

im-mor-tal-i-ty. Here in the bo-dy pent, Absent from Him I roam, Yet nightly pitch my

moving tent A day's march nearer home, nearer home, near-er home, A day's march nearer home.

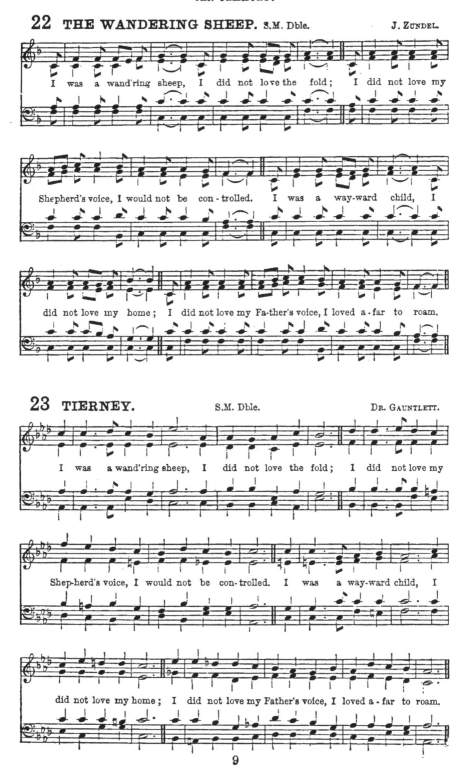

22 **THE WANDERING SHEEP.** S.M. Dble.   J. ZUNDEL.

I was a wand'ring sheep, I did not love the fold; I did not love my

Shepherd's voice, I would not be con - trolled. I was a way-ward child, I

did not love my home; I did not love my Fa-ther's voice, I loved a - far to roam.

23 **TIERNEY.**   S.M. Dble.   DR. GAUNTLETT.

I was a wand'ring sheep, I did not love the fold; I did not love my

Shep-herd's voice, I would not be con-trolled. I was a way-ward child, I

did not love my home; I did not love my Father's voice, I loved a - far to roam.

24 ARNOLD'S. *   C.M.   DR. ARNOLD.

Je - sus, I love Thy charm - ing name, 'Tis mu - sic to my ear;

Fain would I sound it out so loud, That earth and heaven should hear.

25 BEDFORD.   C.M.   W. WHEALL.

O God of Beth - el! by whose hand Thy peo - ple still are fed;

Who through this earth - ly pil - grim - age Hast all our fa - thers led.

26 BELMONT. *   C.M.   S. WEBBE.

Je - sus, the ve - ry thought of Thee, With sweet - ness fills my breast;

But sweet - er far Thy face to see, And in Thy pres - ence rest.

27 BYZANTIUM. *

C.M. JACKSON. Arrangement from "The Hymnary," by per.

Come, Chris-tian chil-dren, come and raise Your voice with one ac-cord;

Come, sing in joy-ful songs of praise The glo-ries of your Lord.

28 CLARABELLA.

C.M. From MAJOR's "Tunes and Chants for Home and School."

There's not a tint that paints the rose, Or decks the li - ly fair,

Or streaks the hum-blest flower that blows, But God has placed it there.

29 DALEHURST.

C.M. ARTHUR COTTMAN.

There is a heaven of per-fect peace, Th'e-ter-nal throne is there;

But what that tear-less re-gion is It doth not yet ap-pear.

30 EVAN. C.M. Rev. W. H. Havergal.

Ye hearts, with youth - ful vig - our warm, In smil - ing crowds draw near;

And turn from ev - 'ry mor - tal charm A Sa-viour's voice to hear.

31 EVANGELIST. C.M. From Mendelssohn.

Sing to the Lord the chil-dren's hymn, His gen - tle love de - clare,

Who bends a - mid the ser - a - phim To hear the chil-dren's prayer.

32 FARRANT. C.M. R. Farrant.

There is a path that leads to God, All o - thers lead a - stray;

Nar - row but plea - sant is the road, And Chris - tians love the way.

33 HAVANNAH. * C.M. DR. HARRINGTON. From "The Psalmist," by per.

Come, Ho - ly Ghost the Com - fort - er, Whom Je - sus sends from heaven,

O com - fort us, Thy chil - dren here, And show our sins for-given.

34 HOLSTEIN. C.M. From WEBER. From "The School Hymnal Tune Book," by permission.

Hap - py the child whose youngest years Re - ceive in - struc - tion well;

Who hates the sin - ner's path, and fears The road that leads to hell.

35 HORSLEY. C.M. W. HORSLEY, Mus. Bac.

There is a green hill far a - way, With - out a ci - ty wall,

Where the dear Lord was cru - ci - fied, Who died to save us all.

13

36 IRISH. C.M. ISAAC SMITH.

How soft-ly on the west-ern hills, The sun-set light is shed!

So Christ the Lord sheds forth His peace A-round the dy-ing bed.

37 LÆTITIA. C.M. From SILCHER. From the "St. Alban's Tune Book."

There is a name I love to hear, I love to speak its worth;

It sounds like mu-sic in mine ear, The sweet-est name on earth.

38 LONDON NEW. * C.M. Arrangement from "The Hymnary," by per. DR. CROFT.

O for a shout of sa-cred joy To God, the sov-'reign King!

Let ev-'ry land its tongues em-ploy, And hymns of tri-umph sing.

14

39 MANCHESTER. *   C.M.   Dr. Wainwright.

'Tis but a veil that hangs be- tween The saint and joys di - ' vine,

And beams of glo - ry oft are seen A - midst its folds to shine.

40 MANOAH.   C.M.   From Rossini.

I love to think, tho' I am young, My Sa - viour was a child ;

That Je - sus walked this earth a - long, With feet all un - de - filed.

41 MARLOW.   C.M.   Adapted by Dr. Mason.
From "Congregational Church Music."

Oh, it is hard to work for God, To rise and take His part,

Up on this bat - tle - field of earth, And not some times lose heart.

15

42 MARTYRDOM. * C.M. HUGH WILSON.

Do not I love Thee, O my Lord? Be - hold my heart and see,

And turn each cher - ished i - dol out That dares to ri - val Thee.

43 MILES' LANE. * C.M.P. SHRUBSOLE.

All hail the pow'r of Je - su's name, Let an - gels prostrate fall; Bring forth the Roy-al

Di - a - dem, And crown Him, crown Him, crown Him, crown Him Lord of all.

44 NAZARETH. C.M. T. WALLHEAD.

God might have made the earth bring forth E - nough for great and small,

The oak tree and the ce - dar tree, With - out a flow'r at all.

45 OLD WINCHESTER. * C.M.   ESTE's Psalter.

This is the day the Lord hath made, He calls the hours His own,

Let heav'n re-joice, let earth be glad, And praise sur-round the throne.

46 PHILIPPI. *   C.M.   S. WESLEY.
From "The Psalmist," by per.

My God, ac-cept my heart this day, And make it al-ways Thine,

That I from Thee no more may stray, No more from Thee de-cline.

47 RICHMOND.   C.M.   REV. DR. HAWEIS.
From "Congregational Church Music."

Je-sus, the Friend of friend-less men, The help of all the weak;

Je-sus, who left the joys of heaven The lost and sad to seek.

48 ST. ANN'S. *   C.M.   DR. CROFT.

The Sa-viour calls; let ev-'ry ear At-tend the heav'n-ly sound:

Ye doubt-ing ones, dis-miss your fear; Hope smiles re-viv-ing round.

49 ST. JAMES.   C.M.   COURTEVILLE.
From "Congregational Church Music."

How glo-rious is our heav'n-ly King, Who reigns a-bove the sky!

How shall a child pre-sume to sing His dread-ful ma-jes-ty!

50 ST. MAGNUS.   C.M.   J. CLARK.

Come, hap-py chil-dren, come and raise Your voice with one ac-cord;

Come, sing a cheer-ful song of praise, And bless your Sa-viour Lord.

51 ST. PETER.   C.M.   A. R. REINAGLE.

How sweet the name of Je - sus sounds In a be - liev - er's ear!

It soothes his sor - row, heals his wounds, And drives a - way his fear.

52 ST. SAVIOUR.   C.M.   F. G. BAKER.

Hark the glad sound, the Sa - viour comes! The Sa - viour pro - mised long!

Let ev' - ry heart pre - pare a throne, And ev' - ry voice a song.

53 ST. STEPHEN. *   C.M.   REV. W. JONES.

I sing th'al - migh - ty pow'r of God That made the moun - tains rise,

That spread the flow - ing seas a - broad, And built the lof - ty skies.

19

54 SAWLEY. C.M. J. WALCH.

Lord, give me light to do thy work, For on - ly, Lord, from Thee

Org.

Can come the light by which these eyes The work of truth can see.

Org.

55 SOLOMON. C.M. From HANDEL.

The gold - en gates are lift - ed up, The doors are o - pen wide,

The King of Glo - ry is gone in, Un - to His Fa - ther's side.

56 TALLIS. C.M. TALLIS.

Al - migh - ty God, Thy pierc - ing eye Strikes through the shades of night,

And our most se - cret ac - tions lie All o - pen to Thy sight.

57 TIVERTON. C.M. GRIGG.

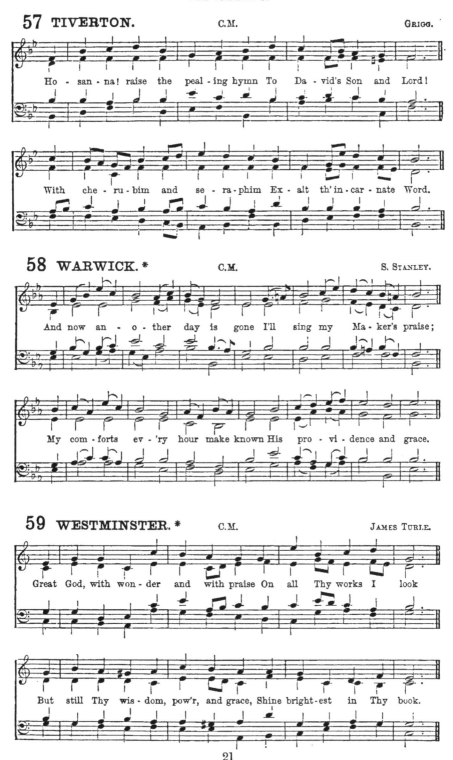

Ho - san - na! raise the peal - ing hymn To Da - vid's Son and Lord!

With che - ru - bim and se - ra - phim Ex - alt th' in - car - nate Word.

58 WARWICK. * C.M. S. STANLEY.

And now an - o - ther day is gone I'll sing my Ma - ker's praise;

My com - forts ev - 'ry hour make known His pro - vi - dence and grace.

59 WESTMINSTER. * C.M. JAMES TURLE.

Great God, with won - der and with praise On all Thy works I look

But still Thy wis - dom, pow'r, and grace, Shine bright - est in Thy book.

60 ANNIVERSARY. C.M., with Chorus.

W. B. BRADBURY.

A year a-gain has passed away, Time swiftly speeds a - long; We come a -gain to praise and pray, And sing our greeting song. We come,......... We come,...... We come with song to greet you, We come,......... We come,...... We come with song a - gain.

We come, We come, We come, We come,

We come, We come, We come, We come,

61 GLORY. C.M., with Refrain.

A - round the throne of God in heav'n Thou-sands of chil - dren stand;

Chil - dren whose sins are all for - giv'n, A ho - ly, hap - py band,

REFRAIN.

Sing-ing glo - ry, glo - ry, glo - ry, Sing-ing glo - ry, glo - ry, glo - ry.

62 GLORY. C.M., with Refrain.

A-round the throne of God in heav'n Thousands of chil-dren stand ; Chil-dren whose sins are

REFRAIN.

all forgiv'n, A ho - ly, hap-py band, Singing glo-ry, glo-ry, Glo-ry be to God on high.

63 CHILDREN'S JUBILEE. C.M., with Chorus. By permission of the Sunday School Union.

Ho - san - na, ho-san - na, ho - san - na ! Ho-san - na be the children's song, To

Christ the children's King : His praise to whom their souls belong, Let all the chil-dren sing.

CHORUS.

Ho - san - na then our song shall be, Ho - san - na to our King ! This is the children's

FULL CHORUS.

ju - bi lee : Let all the children sing. This is the children's ju-bi-lee ; Let all the chil-dren sing.

64 HEAVEN.

C.M., with Chorus.

We're marching to the pro-mised land, A land all fair and bright; Come, join our

hap-py youth-ful band And seek the plains of light. We're march-ing thro' Im-

-man-uel's ground, And soon shall hear the trum-pet sound; And there we

GIRLS.

shall with Je-sus reign, And nev-er, nev-er part a-gain. What, nev-er part a-

BOYS.   GIRLS.   BOYS.

-gain? No, nev-er part a-gain. What, nev-er part a-gain? No, nev-er part a-

ALL.

-gain; And there we shall with Je-sus reign, And nev-er, nev-er part a-gain.

65 SPOHR. * 6 lines, 8.6. From Spohr.

Dis - miss me not Thy ser - vice, Lord, But train me for Thy will;

For ev - en I in fields so broad, Some du - ties may ful - fil;

First termination. | *Second termination.*

And I will ask for no re - ward, Ex - cept to serve Thee still. -cept to serve Thee still.

66 REDEMPTION. 8.6.8.6.8.8.8. P. R. Richards. From "The Methodist Sunday School Tune Book," by per.

Ten thousand times ten thousand sung Their anthems round the throne, When lo! one so - li -

- ta - ry tongue Be - gan a song un - known; A song un-known to an - gels' ears, A

song that spoke of ban-ished fears, Of par - doned sins, of dried - up tears.

67 O PARADISE.   8.6.8.6.6.6.6.6.

HEMY. Harmonized by J. T. COOPER.
By permission of MR. H. C. HEMY,
Newcastle-on-Tyne.

68 PARADISE.   8.6.8.6.6.6.6.6.C.   JOHN GILL.

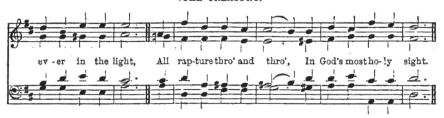

ev - er in the light, All rap-ture thro' and thro', In God's most ho-!y sight.

69 ST. WINIFRED. C.M. or 8.8.8.6., with Refrain. REV. R. LOWRY.

There is a clime where Je - sus reigns, A home of peace and love, Where

an - gels wait with sweetest strains To greet the saints a - bove. They'll sing their wel-come

home to me, They'll sing their wel-come home to me; The an - gels will stand On the

heav'n-ly strand, And sing their wel- come home. Wel -come home, Wel - come home.

The an - gels will stand On the heav'n-ly strand, And sing their wel - come home.

70 AULD LANG SYNE. 12 lines, 8.6.   Scotch.

Hail! sweet-est, dear-est tie that binds Our glow-ing hearts in one;

Hail! sa-cred hope that tunes our minds To har-mo-ny di-vine.

It is the hope, the bliss-ful hope, Which Je-sus' grace has given;

The hope when days and years are past We all shall meet in heaven.

We all shall meet in heaven at last, We all shall meet in heaven;

The hope when days and years are past We all shall meet in heaven.

71 SWEET SABBATH SCHOOL. C.M., with Chorus.   W. H. DOANE.

Sweet Sab-bath School! more dear to me Than fair-est pa-lace dome,

My heart e'er turns with joy to thee, My own dear Sab-bath Home.

CHORUS.

Sab-bath Home!   Bless-èd Home!   Sab-bath Home!   Bless-èd

Sweet Home!   Sweet Home!   Sweet Home!

Home!   My heart e'er turns with joy to thee, My own dear Sab-bath Home.

Sweet Home!

72 RETURN, O WANDERER. C.M., with Refrain.

Re-turn, O wan-d'rer, to thy home, Thy Fa-ther calls for thee;

No long-er now an ex-ile roam, In guilt and mis-e-ry. Re-turn, Re-turn!

73 AUDITE AUDIENTES ME. C.M., Dble. Dr. A. Sullivan.

VOICES IN UNISON.

Org.

I heard the voice of Je - sus say, "Come un - to Me, and rest;

Lay down, poor wea - ry one, lay down Thy head up - on My breast:"

VOICES IN HARMONY. *cres.*

I came to Je - sus as I was, Wea - ry and worn and sad;
2nd and 3rd Verses—and I drank Of that life - giv - ing stream;

I found in Him a rest - ing - place, And He has made me glad.

74 ELLACOMBE. C.M., Dble. German.

The Son of God goes forth to war, A king - ly crown to gain;

His blood - red ban - ner streams a - far: Who fol - lows in His train?

Who best can drink His cup of woe, Tri - umph - ant o - ver pain;

Who pa - tient bears His cross be - low, He fol - lows in His train.

75 LAND OF REST. C.M., Dble. R. S. Newman.

The ro - seate hues of ear - ly dawn, The bright - ness of the day,

The crim - son of the sun - set sky, How fast they fade a - way!

Oh, for the pearl - y gates of heaven! Oh, for the gold - en floor!

Oh, for the Sun of Righ - teous - ness That set - teth ne - ver - more.

76 NOEL. C.M., Dble. Arranged by Dr. A. Sullivan.

It came up - on the mid - night clear, That glo - rious song of old,

From au - gels bend - ing near the earth, To touch the harps of gold—

"Peace to the earth, good - will to men, From heaven's all - gra - cious King!"

A little slower. *pp*

The world in so - lemn still-ness lay To hear the an - gels sing.

77 PALESTINE. * C.M., Dble.

O hap - py land! O hap - py land! Where saints and an - gels dwell,

We long to join that glo - rious band, And all their an - thems swell.

But ev - 'ry voice in yon - der throng On earth has breathed a prayer;

No lips un - taught may join that song, Or learn the mu - sic there.

78 PROSPECT.*   C.M., Dble.   Old English Air.

There is a land of pure de - light, Where saints im - mor - tal reign;

In - fi - nite day ex - cludes the night, And plea - sures ban - ish pain.

There ev - er - last - ing spring a - bides, And nev - er - with - 'ring flowers;

Death, like a nar - row sea, di - vides This heaven - ly land from ours.

79 ST. MATTHEW. * C.M., Dble.   DR. CROFT.

The Ga - li - le - an fish - ers toil All night, and no - thing take:

But Je - sus comes— a won - drous spoil Is lift - ed from the lake!

Lord, when our la - bours are in vain, And vain the help of men,

When fruit - less is our care and pain, Come, bless - ed Je - sus, then!

80 SPES CELESTIS.   C.M., Dble.   W. A. SMITH.

While shep - herds watch'd their flocks by night, All seat - ed on the ground,

The an - gel of the Lord came down, And glo - ry shone a - round.

"Fear not!" said he, for migh - ty dread Had seized their trou - bled mind;

"Glad ti - dings of great joy I bring To you and all man - kind."

81 THERE IS A GREEN HILL. C.M., with Refrain. R. S. WILLIS.

There is a green hill far a - way, With - out a ci - ty wall,

Where the dear Lord was cru - ci - fied, Who died to save us all.

REFRAIN.

Oh, dear - ly, dear - ly has He loved; And we must love Him too,

And trust in His re - deem - ing blood, And try His works to do.

82 CHRISTMAS BELLS. C.M., Dble., with Refrain. J. J. ATACK.

From "The Methodist Sunday School Tune Book," by per.

Ring, ring the bells, the joy ful bells, This mer - ry Christ-mas morn!

Their sweet, me - lo - dious mu - sic tells The day when Christ was born.

Sweet - ly they sound o'er vale and glen; Hark! how their mu - sic swells

With "Peace on earth, good - will to men!" O mer - ry Christ-mas bells!

REFRAIN.

Ring, ring the bells, the Christ-mas bells, The bells, the mer- ry, mer-ry Christmas bells;

Ring, ring the

Christ - - mas bells!

Ring, ring the mer - ry, mer - ry, mer - ry Christ -mas bells!
Ring, ring, ring, ring, Christ - mas bells!

Ring the mer - ry Christ - mas bells!

83 ANGELUS.   L.M.   J. Scheffler.

At e - ven, when the sun was set, The sick, O Lord, a - round Thee lay:

Oh, with what di - vers pains they met! Oh, with what joy they went a - way!

84 BEETHOVEN. *   L.M.   From Beethoven.

Go la - bour on; spend and be spent; Thy joy to do the Fa - ther's will:

It is the way the Mas - ter went; Should not the ser - vant tread it still?

85 BOSTON.   L.M.   Arranged by Dr. L. Mason.

I would a youth - ful pil - grim be, Re - solved a - lone to fol - low Thee;

Thou Lamb of God, who now art gone Up to Thine ev - er - last - ing throne.

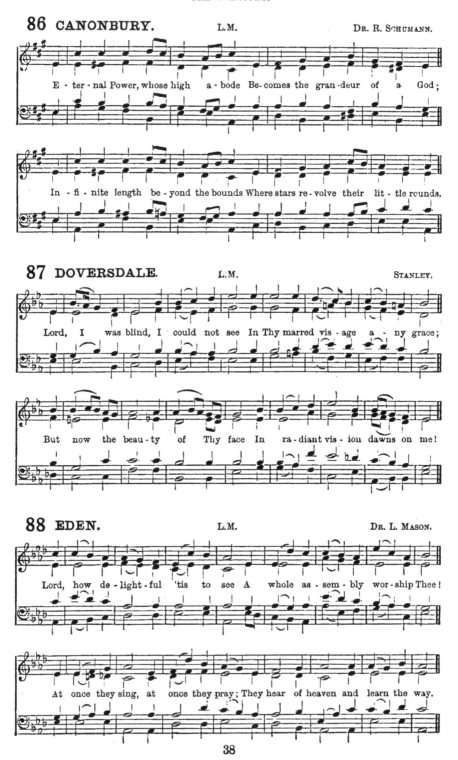

86 CANONBURY.   L.M.   Dr. R. Schumann.

E - ter - nal Power, whose high a - bode Be - comes the gran - deur of a God;

In - fi - nite length be - yond the bounds Where stars re - volve their lit - tle rounds.

87 DOVERSDALE.   L.M.   Stanley.

Lord, I was blind, I could not see In Thy marred vis - age a - ny grace;

But now the beau - ty of Thy face In ra - diant vis - ion dawns on me!

88 EDEN.   L.M.   Dr. L. Mason.

Lord, how de - light - ful 'tis to see A whole as - sem - bly wor - ship Thee!

At once they sing, at once they pray; They hear of heaven and learn the way.

89 EISENACH. * L.M. J. H. SCHEIN. Arranged by W. C. FILBY.

When Is-rael thro' the de-sert passed A fie-ry pil-lar went be-fore,

To guide them thro' the drea-ry waste, And less-en the fa-tigues they bore.

90 ERNAN. L.M. DR. L. MASON.

Oh, do not let the word de-part, Nor close thine eyes a-gainst the light!

Con-vict-ed youth, steel not thy heart: Thou wouldst be saved—why not to-night?

91 EVENING HYMN. L.M. T. TALLIS.

Glo-ry to Thee, my God, this night, For all the bless-ings of the light;

Keep me, oh, keep me, King of kings, Be-neath Thine own al-migh-ty wings.

92 GIBRALTAR. L.M. C. W. POOLE.

From year to year in love we meet, From year to year in peace we part,

The tongues of chil-dren ut-t'ring sweet The bo-som-joy of ev-'ry heart.

93 HOLLEY. L.M. GEORGE HEWS.

Lord, speak to me, that I may speak In liv-ing e-choes of Thy tone;

As Thou hast sought, so let me seek Thy err-ing chil-dren, lost and lone.

94 HONITON. L.M. JOHN HATTON.

O hap-py day, that fixed my choice On Thee, my Sa-viour and my God!

Well may this glow-ing heart re-joice, And tell its rap-tures all a-broad.

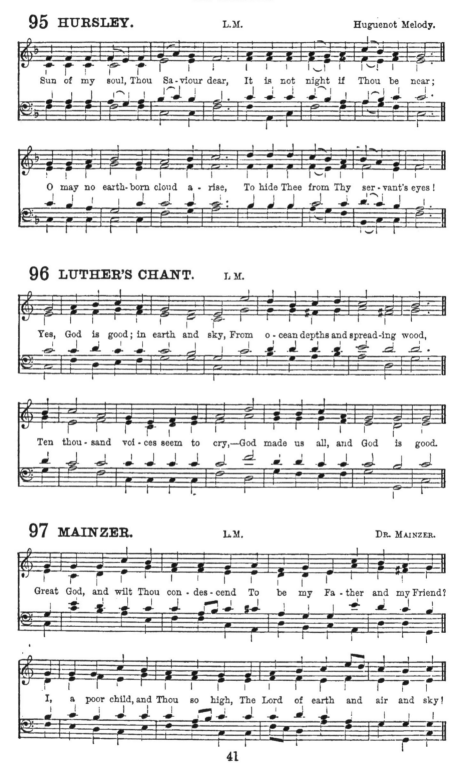

95 HURSLEY.   L.M.   Huguenot Melody.

Sun of my soul, Thou Sa-viour dear, It is not night if Thou be near;

O may no earth-born cloud a-rise, To hide Thee from Thy ser-vant's eyes!

96 LUTHER'S CHANT.   L M.

Yes, God is good; in earth and sky, From o-cean depths and spread-ing wood,

Ten thou-sand voi-ces seem to cry,—God made us all, and God is good.

97 MAINZER.   L.M.   DR. MAINZER.

Great God, and wilt Thou con-des-cend To be my Fa-ther and my Friend?

I, a poor child, and Thou so high, The Lord of earth and air and sky!

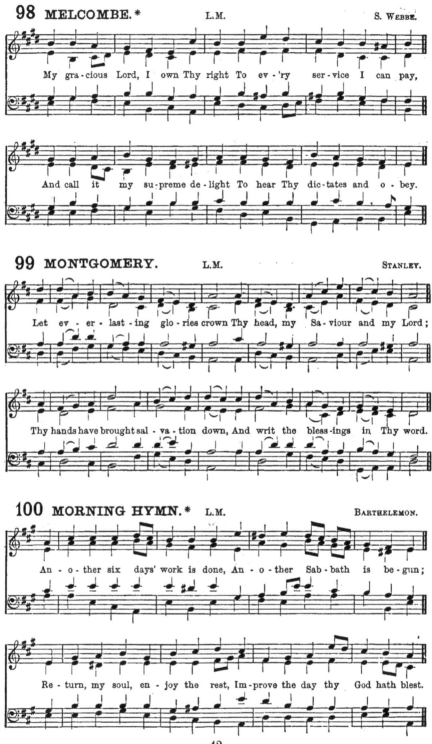

98 MELCOMBE.*　　　L.M.　　　S. WEBBE.

My gra-cious Lord, I own Thy right To ev-'ry ser-vice I can pay,

And call it my su-preme de-light To hear Thy dic-tates and o-bey.

99 MONTGOMERY.　　　L.M.　　　STANLEY.

Let ev-er-last-ing glo-ries crown Thy head, my Sa-viour and my Lord;

Thy hands have brought sal-va-tion down, And writ the bless-ings in Thy word.

100 MORNING HYMN.*　　　L.M.　　　BARTHELEMON.

An-o-ther six days' work is done, An-o-ther Sab-bath is be-gun;

Re-turn, my soul, en-joy the rest, Im-prove the day thy God hath blest.

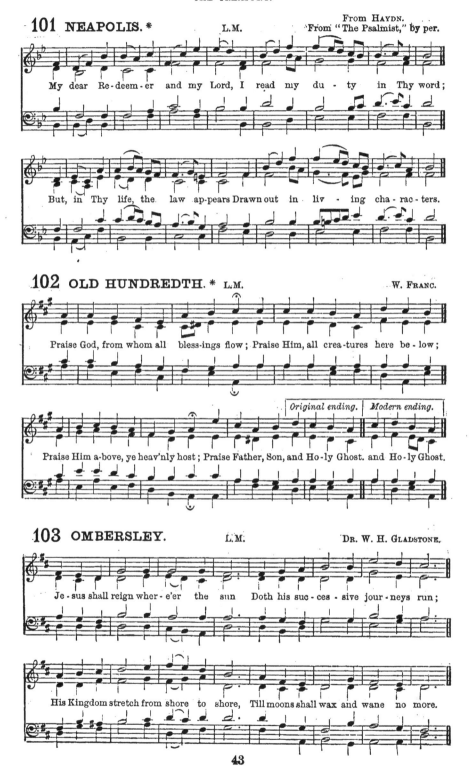

101 NEAPOLIS. *　　　　　L.M.　　　From HAYDN.
From "The Psalmist," by per.

My dear Re-deem-er and my Lord, I read my du-ty in Thy word;

But, in Thy life, the law ap-pears Drawn out in liv-ing cha-rac-ters.

102 OLD HUNDREDTH. * L.M.　　　　　W. FRANC.

Praise God, from whom all bless-ings flow; Praise Him, all crea-tures here be-low;

Original ending. | Modern ending.

Praise Him a-bove, ye heav'nly host; Praise Father, Son, and Ho-ly Ghost. and Ho-ly Ghost.

103 OMBERSLEY.　　　　L.M.　　　DR. W. H. GLADSTONE.

Je-sus shall reign wher-e'er the sun Doth his suc-ces-sive jour-neys run;

His Kingdom stretch from shore to shore, Till moons shall wax and wane no more.

104 ROCKINGHAM (CATON). L.M.   DR. MILLER.

O time - ly hap - py, time - ly wise, Hearts that with ris - ing morn a - rise!

Eyes that the beam ce - les - tial view, Which ev - er - more makes all things new!

105 SAMSON.   L.M.   From HANDEL.

O Lord of Glo - ry! be my Light, Shine as my guid - ing star on high;

Rise al - so as a star with - in, That I may know Thee al - ways nigh.

106 SIMEON.   L.M.   S. STANLEY.

Sing to the Lord a joy - ful song, Lift up your hearts, your voi - ces raise:

To us His gra-cious gifts be - long, To Him our songs of love and praise.

107 WANDSWORTH. L.M.

W. BEALE.
From " The Psalmist," by per.

Stand up, my soul, shake off thy fears, And gird the gos - pel ar - mour on;

March to the gates of end - less joy, Where thy great Cap - tain - Sa - viour's gone.

108 WARRINGTON. L.M.

REV. R. HARRISON.

Tri - umph-ant, Lord, Thy good - ness reigns Thro' all the wide ce - les - tial plains;

And its full streams re - dund - ant flow Down to th'a - bodes of men be - low.

109 WHITBURN. L.M.

H. BAKER, MUS. BAC.

When to the house of God we go, To hear His word, and sing His love,

We ought to wor - ship Him be - low, As saints and an - gels do a - bove.

110 WINCHESTER. *   L.M.   CRASSELIUS.

From all that dwell be - low the skies, Let the Cre - a - tor's praise a - rise;

Let the Re - deem - er's name be sung Thro' ev - 'ry land, by ev - 'ry tongue.

111 WOOLSTANTON. *   L.M.   E. HAWKINS. From "The Psalmist," by per.

From ev - 'ry storm - y wind that blows, From ev - 'ry swell - ing tide of woes,

There is a calm, a safe re - treat; 'Tis found be - neath the mer - cy - seat.

112 ANNIVERSARY SONG. L.M., with Refrain.   W. F. SHERWIN.

We sing our song of ju - bi - lee, Our voi - ces ris - ing loud and free;

And with the notes of sweet ac - cord We praise our ev - er - bless - ed Lord.

113 CREATION. L.M., Dble. From HAYDN.

The spa-cious fir-ma-ment on high, With all the blue e-the-real sky,

And spangled heavens, a shin-ing frame, Their great O-ri-gi-nal pro-claim;

Th' un-wea-ried sun, from day to day, Does his Cre-a-tor's power dis-play,

And pub-lish-es to ev-'ry land The work of an Al-migh-ty hand.

114 SWEET HOUR OF PRAYER. L.M., Dble.

W. B. BRADBURY.

Moderato.

Sweet hour of prayer! sweet hour of prayer! That calls me from a world of care,

And bids me at my Fa-ther's throne Make all my wants and wish-es known.

In sea-sons of dis-tress and grief My soul has of-ten found re-lief,

And oft es-caped the tempt-er's snare, By thy re-turn, sweet hour of prayer!

115 STAND UP FOR JESUS.
L.M., with Chorus.

From MAJOR'S " Tunes and Chants for Home and School."

Stand up for Je-sus, Chris-tian, stand! Firm as a rock on o-cean's strand!

Beat back the waves of sin that roll, Like rag-ing floods, a-round the soul.

CHORUS.

Stand up for Je - sus, no - bly stand! Firm as a rock on o - cean's strand!

Stand up! His righ-teous cause de - fend, Stand up for Je - sus, your best friend!

116 O HAPPY DAY. L.M., with Chorus.

O hap-py day, that fixed my choice On Thee, my Sa - viour and my God! Well may this

CHORUS.

glow-ing heart re - joice, And tell its rap-tures all a - broad. Hap- py day! hap - py day!

When Je-sus washed my sins a - way! He taught me how to watch and pray, And live re -

- joic - ing ev 'ry day; Hap-py day! hap-py day! When Jesus washed my sins a - way!

117 BLUNTISHAM. 4.10.10.10.4.

Come, la - bour on: { Who dares / stand idle on } the har - vest plain, { While all around / him waves the }

gold - en grain, { And every / servant hears } the Mas - ter say, "Go, work to - day"?

118 SOUND THE BATTLE-CRY. 5.5.5.3.5.5.5.4., with Chorus.

W. F. SHERWIN.

Sound the bat - tle cry! See, the foe is nigh; Raise the stand-ard high For the Lord;

Gird your ar - mour on, Stand firm, ev - 'ry one; Rest your cause up - on His

CHORUS.

ho - ly Word. Rouse then, sol - diers! Ral - ly round the ban - ner!

Stea - dy, stea - dy, pass the word a - long, On - ward, for - ward,

119 WINCHCOMBE. 5.5.5.11. DR. H. HILES.

cres.

O Je-sus! be-hold The lambs of Thy fold, Who join in Thy praise, And sing Hal-le-

a poco rit.

-lu-jah in rap-tur-ous lays, And sing Hal-le-lu-jah in rap-tur-ous lays.

120 HARWICH.* 5.5.11.5.5.11. MILGROVE.

All ye that pass by, To Je-sus draw nigh; To you is it

no-thing that Je-sus should die? Your ran-som and peace, Your

sure-ty He is: Come, see if there ev-er was sor-row like His.

121 HOSANNA. 5.5.5.11., Dble. DR. GAUNTLETT.

All thanks be to God, Who scat-ters a - broad, Through-out ev - 'ry

place, By the means of His ser-vants, His sa - vour of grace: Who the vic - to - ry

gave, The praise let Him have For the work He has

done, All glo - ry and hon - our to Je - sus a - lone.

122 ST. HILDA. 5.6.6.4. R. TOMLINSON.

Moderato.

God, who made the earth, The air, the sky, the sea,

Who gave the light its birth, Car - eth for me.

123 **O SING TO THE LORD.** 5.5.8.6.6.8.   A. RHODES, R.A.M.

From " The Methodist Sunday School Tune Book," by per.

O sing to the Lord In joy - ous ac - cord, Ye dwell - ers on

earth and in heaven; The God of cre - a - tion, The God of sal - va - tion, To

Him all the glo - ry be given! To Him all the glo - ry be given!

124 **EMMELINE.**   8 lines, 5.6.   DR. H. T. LESLIE. From "Tunes and Chants for Home and School."

God in - trusts to all Ta - lents few or ma - ny; None so young or

small That they have not a - ny. Though the great and wise Have a lar - ger

num - ber, Yet my one I prize, And it must not slum - ber.

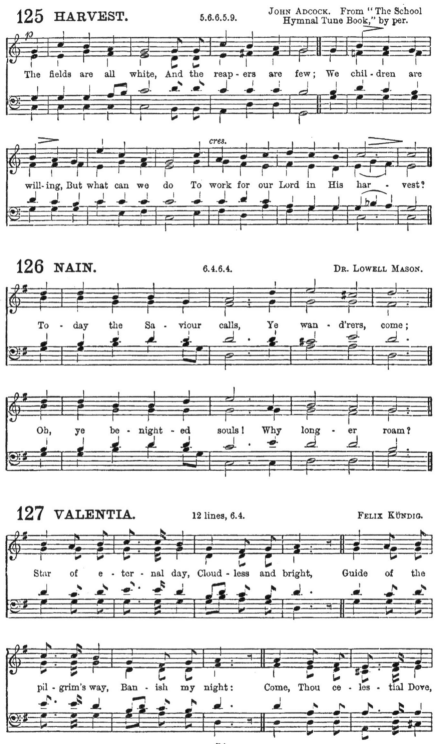

125 HARVEST. 5.6.6.5.9.   JOHN ADCOCK. From "The School Hymnal Tune Book," by per.

The fields are all white, And the reap-ers are few; We chil-dren are will-ing, But what can we do To work for our Lord in His har - vest?

cres.

126 NAIN. 6.4.6.4.   DR. LOWELL MASON.

To - day the Sa - viour calls, Ye wan - d'rers, come; Oh, ye be - night - ed souls! Why long - er roam?

127 VALENTIA. 12 lines, 6.4.   FELIX KÜNDIG.

Star of e - ter - nal day, Cloud - less and bright, Guide of the pil - grim's way, Ban - ish my night: Come, Thou ce - les - tial Dove,

Dwell in my heart; Source of im - mor - tal love, Nev - er de -

part .... Oh, how I long for Thee, Spi - rit di - vine!

What is the world to me?— Je - sus is mine!

128 SAVIOUR, THY DYING LOVE. 6.4.6.4.6.6.6.4.   R. Lowry.

Sa - viour, Thy dy - ing love Thou gav - est me! Nor should I

ought with - hold, Dear Lord, from Thee; In love my soul would bow,

My heart ful - fil its vow, Some off - 'ring bring Thee now, Some-thing for Thee.

129 BEULAH.   6.4.6.4.6.6.6.4.   DR. LOWELL MASON.

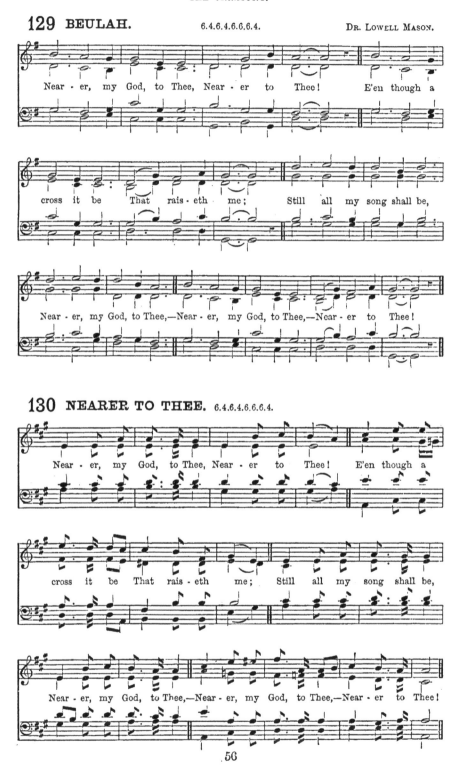

Near - er, my God, to Thee, Near - er to Thee! E'en though a

cross it be That rais - eth me; Still all my song shall be,

Near - er, my God, to Thee,—Near - er, my God, to Thee,—Near - er to Thee!

130 NEARER TO THEE. 6.4.6.4.6.6.6.4.

Near - er, my God, to Thee, Near - er to Thee! E'en though a

cross it be That rais - eth me; Still all my song shall be,

Near - er, my God, to Thee,—Near - er, my God, to Thee,—Near - er to Thee!

131 INDIANA. *　　　　6.4.6.4.6.7.6.4.

There is a hap-py land, Far, far a-way, Where saints in glo-ry stand,

Bright, bright as day. Oh, how they sweet-ly sing, Wor-thy is our

Sa-viour King: Loud let His prais-es ring— Praise, praise for aye.

132 BUDLEIGH.　　　　6.4.6.4.10.10.　　　　T. M. MUDIE.

I lift my heart to Thee, Sa-viour di-vine! For Thou art all to

me, And I am Thine. Is there on earth a clos-er bond than

this, That my Be-lov-ed's mine, and I am His?

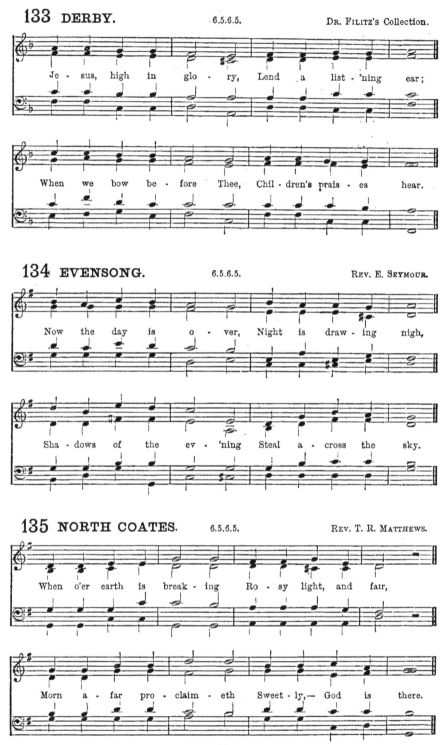

133 DERBY.   6.5.6.5.   Dr. Filitz's Collection.

Je - sus, high in glo - ry, Lend a list - 'ning ear;

When we bow be - fore Thee, Chil - dren's prais - es hear.

134 EVENSONG.   6.5.6.5.   Rev. E. Seymour.

Now the day is o - ver, Night is draw - ing nigh,

Sha - dows of the ev - 'ning Steal a - cross the sky.

135 NORTH COATES.   6.5.6.5.   Rev. T. R. Matthews.

When o'er earth is break - ing Ro - sy light, and fair,

Morn a - far pro - claim - eth Sweet - ly,— God is there.

136 ST. CLOTHILDE.   6.5.6.5.   JAMES SAMPSON.

Lit - tle drops of wa - ter, Lit - tle grains of sand,

Make the migh - ty o - cean, And the beau - teous land.

137 ST. JUDE.   6.5.6.5.   REV. GEO. PETTITT.

I'm a lit - tle pil - grim, And a strang - er here;

Though this world is plea - sant, Sin is al - ways near.

138 ST. LAMBERT.   6.5.6.5.   REV. R. R. CHOPE, B.A.

Ho - ly Spi - rit! hear us; Help us while we sing;

Breathe in - to the mu - sic Of the praise we bring.

139 FRANCONIA.   6.5.6.5., Dble.

At the name of Je - sus   Ev - 'ry knee shall bow,   Ev - 'ry tongue con-

- fess Him   King of Glo - ry now;   'Tis   the Fa - ther's plea - sure

We should call Him Lord,   Who from the be - gin - ning   Was the migh-ty Word.

140 IF I COME TO JESUS. 6.5.6.5., Dble.

If I come to Je - sus,   He will make me glad;   He will give me

plea - sure   When my heart is sad.   If I come to Je - sus,

Hap-py I shall be;   He is gen - tly call - ing   Lit - tle ones like me.

141 JESUS IS OUR SHEPHERD. 6.5.6.5., Dble.

Je - sus is our Shep - herd, Wip - ing ev - 'ry tear; Fold - ed in His

bo - som, What have we to fear? On - ly let us fol - low

Whi - ther He doth lead, To the thirs - ty de - sert, or the dew - y mead.

142 ST. CEPHAS. 6.5.6.5., Dble. REV. H. A. CROSBIE.

In the win - t'ry hea - ven Shines a won-drous star; In the East the

wise men Watched it from a - far; Ask - ing, "What this lus - tre,

So un - earth - ly bright?" Answ'ring, "Christ in glo - ry Comes to earth to-night!"

143 ST. MARY MAGDALENE. 6.5.6.5., Dble.   REV. DR. J. B. DYKES.

144 VESPERS.   6.5.6.5., Dble.   H. A. PROTHERO.

I be-long to Je-sus; 'Twas a hap-py day When His blood most
pre-cious Washed my sins a - way; When His Ho - ly Spi - rit
Changed my heart of stone, Set His mark up - on me, Sealed me for His own.

From the east-ern moun-tains Press-ing on they come, Wise men in their
wis - dom, To His hum - ble home: Stirred by deep de - vo - tion,
Hast-ing from a - far, Ev - er journeying on - ward, Guid-ed by a star.

145 FLEURY. 12 lines, 6.5. French Air.

Sa - viour, bless - ed Sa - viour, Lis - ten whilst we sing,

Hearts and voi - ces rais - ing Prais - es to our King;

All we have to of - fer, All we hope to be,

Bo - dy, soul, and spi - rit, All we yield to Thee.

On - ward, up - ward, heaven - ward, To our ci - ty bright,

Sing - ing as we jour - ney For - ward in - to light.

146 COPPET.   12 lines, 6.5.   REV. CÆSAR MALAN, D.D

Who is on the Lord's side? Who will serve the King? Who will be His help-ers

O - ther lives to bring? Who will leave the world's side? Who will face the foe?

Who is on the Lord's side? Who for Him will go? By Thy call of mer - cy,

By Thy grace di - vine, We are on the Lord's side, Sa - viour, we are Thine!

147 HAYDN. *   12 lines, 6.5.   From HAYDN.

Bright-ly gleams our ban - ner, Point-ing to the sky, Wav-ing wand'rers on - ward

To their home on high. Journeying o'er the de - sert, Glad-ly thus we pray,

And with hearts u - nit - ed   Take our heav'nward way.   Brightly gleams our ban - ner,

Point-ing   to   the   sky,   Wav- ing wand-'rers   on - ward   To their home on high.

148 HERMAS.   12 lines, 6.5.   MISS F. R. HAVERGAL.

Gold - en harps are sound- ing, An - gel voi - ces ring, Pear - ly gates are o - pened—

O - pened for the King ; Christ, the King of   Glo - ry, Je - sus, King of Love,

CHORUS.

Is   gone up   in   tri - umph To His throne a - bove. All His work is end - ed,

Joy - ful - ly we sing, Je - sus hath as - cend - ed ! Glo - ry   to our King.

149 ST. GERTRUDE. 12 lines, 6.5. DR. ARTHUR SULLIVAN.

For - ward! be our watch - word, Steps and voi - ces joined; Seek the things be -

- fore us, Not a look be - hind: Burns the fie - ry pil - lar

At our ar - my's head; Who shall dream of shrink - ing, For our Cap - tain

led? For - ward through the de - sert, Through the toil and

fight: Ca - naan lies be - fore us, Si - on beams with light.

150 RUTH. 12 lines, 6.5. SAMUEL SMITH.

Earth be-low is teem - ing, Heav'n is bright a - bove; Ev - 'ry brow is beam - ing

In the light of love; Ev - 'ry eye re - joi . ces Ev - 'ry thought is praise;

Slower and more devoutly.

Hap - py hearts and voi - ces Glad - den nights and days. O Al - migh - ty Giv - er!

Boun - ti - ful and free, As the joy in har - vest, Joy we be - fore Thee.

151 CROSBY.

6.5.6.5.7.7.6.5.

HUBERT P. MAIN.

O my Sa - viour, hear me, Draw me close to Thee; Thou hast paid my ran - som,

Thou hast died for me; Now by sim - ple faith I claim Par - don through Thy

gra - cious name; Thou, my Ark of safe - ty, Let me fly to Thee.

152 STRIKE FOR VICTORY. 6.5.6.5.6.5.6.5., with Chorus. W. H. DOANE.

Strike, O strike for vic - t'ry, Sol - diers of the Lord, Hop - ing in His

mer - cy, Trust - ing in His Word: Lift the Gos - pel ban - ner,

High a - bove the world; Let its folds of beau - ty Ev - er be un-

CHORUS.

- furled. Strike, strike for vic - t'ry, He - roes bold;

Strike till the vic - t'ry you be - hold. Strike! strike for

vic- t'ry, ne'er give o'er; Rest then in glo - ry ev - er - more.

153 CHRIST AROSE. 6.5.6.4., with Refrain.

REV. R. LOWRY.

1. Low in the grave He lay, Je - sus, my Sa - viour! Wait - ing the com - ing day,
2. Vain - ly they watch His bed, Je - sus, my Sa - viour! Vain - ly they seal the dead,
3. Death can - not keep his prey, Je - sus, my Sa - viour! He tore the bars a - way,

REFRAIN. *Faster.*

Je - sus, my Lord! Up from the grave He a - rose, With a

He a - rose,

migh - ty tri - umph o'er His foes; He a - rose a Vic - tor from the

He a - rose,

dark do - main, And He lives for ev - er with His saints to reign; He a -

- rose, He a - rose, Al - le - lu - ia! Christ a - rose!

He a - rose, He a - rose,

154 BLANDFORD.　　　6.6.4.6.6.6.4.　　　　　　　　S. WESLEY.

God bless our Sun-day School, In-crease our Sun-day School, God bless our School. Send down Thy

grace di-vine, May ev - 'ry child be Thine, And love all hearts entwine : God bless our School.

155 BROCKLEY.　　　6.6.4.6.6.6.4.　　　　　　　　BRAUN.

Fa - ther of hea-ven, bless Mis-sions with great suc-cess, The work is Thine ! Soon may the

Gos - pel sound Thro' all the world a-round, Till earth's re-mot-est bound To Thee re - sign !

156 MOSCOW. *　　　6.6.4.6.6.6.4.　　　　　　　　FELICE GIARDINI.

Glo-ry to God on high ! Let earth to heaven re - ply,.... Praise ye His name. Angels, His

love a-dore, Who all our sorrows bore ; And saints cry ev - er-more : Worthy the Lamb !

157 NATIONAL ANTHEM. 6.6.4.6.6.6.4.

God bless our na-tive land, May heaven's pro-tect-ing hand Still guard our shore; May peace her

powers ex-tend, Foe be transformed to friend, And Britain's rights de-pend On war no more.

158 NEWHAVEN. * 6.6.4.6.6.6.4.

DR. T. HASTINGS.
Arranged by W. C. FILBY.

Thou, whose al-migh-ty word Cha-os and darkness heard, And took their flight; Hear us, we

hum-bly pray, And where the Gos-pel's day Sheds not its glo-rious ray Let there be light !

159 OLIVET. 6.6.4.6.6.6.4.

DR. LOWELL MASON.

My faith looks up to Thee, Thou Lamb of Cal-va-ry, Sa-viour di-vine! Now hear me

while I pray, Take all my guilt a-way, Oh, may I from this day Be whol-ly Thine.

160 CHRISTINE. 6.4.6.4.6.6.6.4., with Chorus. MISS ABBY HUTCHINSON.

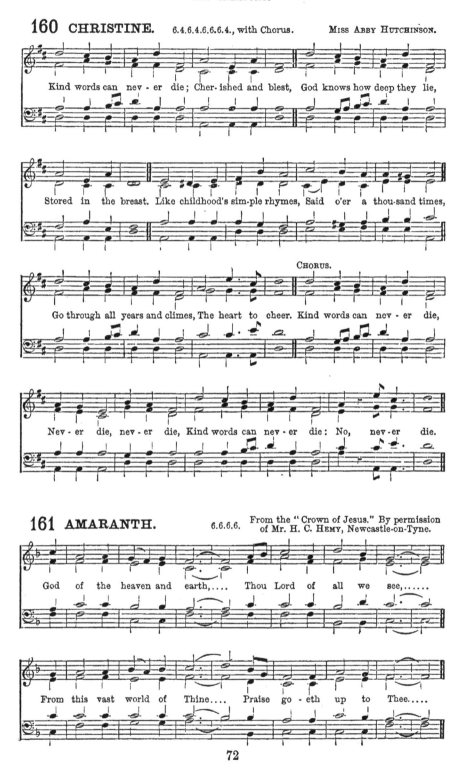

Kind words can nev - er die; Cher- ished and blest, God knows how deep they lie,

Stored in the breast. Like childhood's sim-ple rhymes, Said o'er a thou-sand times,

CHORUS.

Go through all years and climes, The heart to cheer. Kind words can nev - er die,

Nev - er die, nev - er die, Kind words can nev - er die: No, nev-er die.

161 AMARANTH. 6.6.6.6. From the "Crown of Jesus." By permission of Mr. H. C. HEMY, Newcastle-on-Tyne.

God of the heaven and earth,.... Thou Lord of all we see,......

From this vast world of Thine.... Praise go - eth up to Thee.....

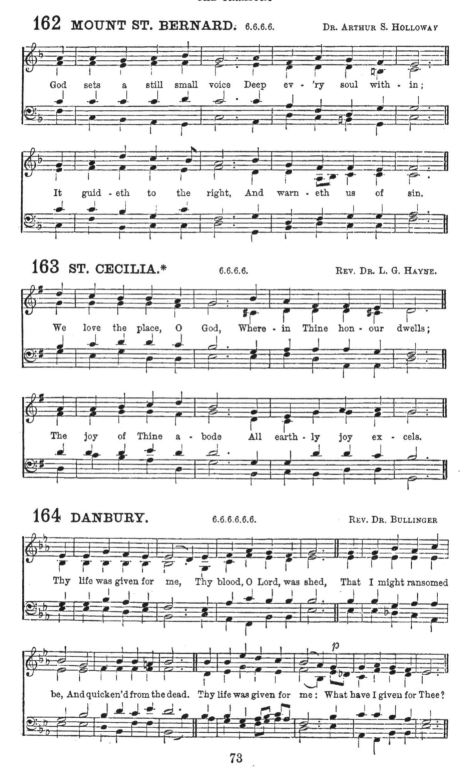

162 MOUNT ST. BERNARD. 6.6.6.6.   Dr. Arthur S. Holloway

God sets a still small voice Deep ev-'ry soul with-in;

It guid-eth to the right, And warn-eth us of sin.

163 ST. CECILIA.* 6.6.6.6.   Rev. Dr. L. G. Hayne.

We love the place, O God, Where-in Thine hon-our dwells;

The joy of Thine a-bode All earth-ly joy ex-cels.

164 DANBURY. 6.6.6.6.6.6.   Rev. Dr. Bullinger

Thy life was given for me, Thy blood, O Lord, was shed, That I might ransomed

be, And quicken'd from the dead. Thy life was given for me: What have I given for Thee?

165 OASIS.   6:6.6.6.6.6.   GEORGE LOMAS, Mus.Bac.

Thy life was given for me, Thy blood, O Lord, was shed, That I might ransom'd be, And quicken'd

from the dead. Thy life was given for me: What have I given for Thee?

166 AGATHA.   8 lines, 6s.   From WEBER.

My Jesus, as Thou wilt! Oh, may Thy will be mine!

Into Thy hand of love, I would my all resign:

Through sorrow or through joy, Conduct me as Thine own,

And help me still to say, My Lord, Thy will be done!

167 BURY ST. EDMUNDS. 8 lines, 6s.   Rev. T. R. Matthews.

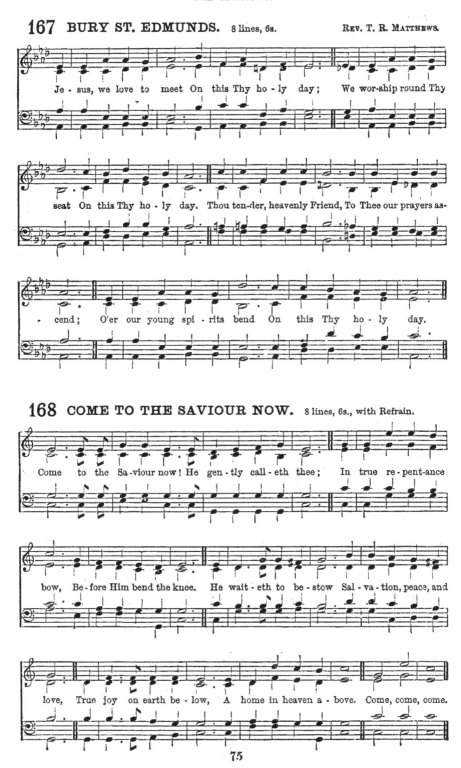

Je - sus, we love to meet On this Thy ho - ly day; We wor-ship round Thy

seat On this Thy ho - ly day. Thou ten-der, heavenly Friend, To Thee our prayers as-

- cend; O'er our young spi - rits bend On this Thy ho - ly day.

168 COME TO THE SAVIOUR NOW. 8 lines, 6s., with Refrain.

Come to the Sa-viour now! He gen-tly call-eth thee; In true re-pent-ance

bow, Be-fore Him bend the knee. He wait-eth to be-stow Sal-va-tion, peace, and

love, True joy on earth be-low, A home in heaven a-bove. Come, come, come.

169 INGLEWHITE. 6.6.8.6.10.12. MRS. MOUNSEY-BARTHOLOMEW.

O Mas - ter, at Thy feet I bow, in rap-ture sweet; Be - fore me, as in dark'ning glass, Some glo -rious out - lines pass Of love and truth, and ho - li - ness and power: I own them Thine, O Christ, and bless Thee for this hour.

170 CHILDREN'S VOICES. 6.6.6.6.4.4.4.4. DR. E. J. HOPKINS.

A - bove the clear blue sky,...... In hea - ven's bright a - bode, The an - gel host on high Sing prais - es to their God: Hal - le - lu - jah! They love to sing To God their King Hal - le - lu - jah!

171 DARWELL'S. *   6.6.6.6.8.8.   REV. J. DARWELL.

Oh, bless the Lord, and praise His gracious, ho-ly name; Let all with-in me raise A tri-bute

to His fame. His mer - cy rests On great and small; Forget not all His ben - e - fits.

172 ECHO SONG.   6.6.6.6.8.8., with Refrain.   W. B. BRADBURY.

Shall hymns of grate-ful love Thro' heaven's high arch-es ring, And all the hosts a -

- bove Their songs of tri-umph sing; And shall not we take up the strain, And

send the e - cho back a - gain? And send the e - cho, send the e - cho, send the e - cho,

send the e - cho, send the e - cho, send the e - cho back a - gain?

173 EXETER (ST. SWITHIN). 6.6.6.6.8.8.   EDWARD JESSER.

Can I, a lit - tle child, Do an - y - thing for those Who are by

sin de - filed To light - en their sad woes? I can - not see the

rea - son why I should not, if I real - ly try.

174 SAFE HOME.   6.6.6.6.8.8.   DR. A. SULLIVAN.

Safe home, safe home in port! Rent cord - age, shat - tered deck,

sails, pro - vi - sion short, And on - ly not a wreck: But

oh, the joy up - on the shore To tell our voy - age - pe - rils o'er!

175 ST. JOHN.   6.6.6.6.8.8.

When lit - tle Sam-uel woke, And heard his Ma-ker's voice, At ev - 'ry word He spoke How

much did he re - joice! O bless-ed, hap - py child, to find The God of heaven so near and kind!

176 SAMUEL.   6.6.6.6.8.8.   DR. A. SULLIVAN.

Hushed was the ev'ning hymn, The temple courts were dark, The lamp was burning dim Be-fore the

sa - cred ark; When sud-den-ly a voice di-vine Rang thro' the si-lence of the shrine.

177 VERBUM PACIS.   6.6.8.4.   GEORGE LOMAS, Mus. Bac.

Reign in my heart, great God, Its throne I leave to Thee;

Oh, let Thy bless - ed law of love Still go - vern me.

178 LAUDAMUS. 6.6.8.4.6.6.8.4. A. B. MERRICK.

The God of A-bra'm praise, Who reigns enthroned a-bove, An-cient of ev-er-

-last-ing days, And God of love! Je-ho-vah, great I AM! By

earth and Heav'n con-fest! We bow and own the sa-cred name, For ev-er blest!

179 INTERCESSION.* 7.5.7.5.7.5.7.5.8.8. W. H. CALLCOTT. Partly from MENDELSSOHN.
By per. of J. NISBET & Co.

When the wea-ry, seek-ing rest, To Thy good-ness flee; When the hea-vy-

-la-den cast All their load on Thee; When the trou-bled, seek-ing peace,

On Thy name shall call; When the sin-ner, seek-ing life,

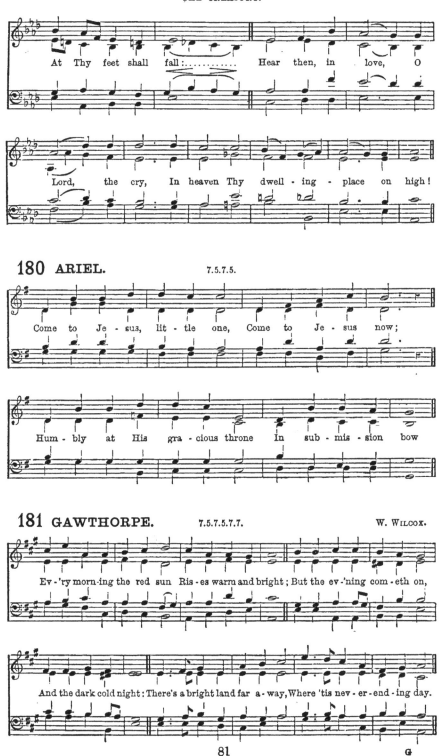

At Thy feet shall fall:............ Hear then, in love, O

Lord, the cry, In heaven Thy dwell - ing - place on high!

180 ARIEL.   7.5.7.5.

Come to Je - sus, lit - tle one, Come to Je - sus now;

Hum - bly at His gra - cious throne In sub - mis - sion bow

181 GAWTHORPE.   7.5.7.5.7.7.   W. WILCOX.

Ev - 'ry morn-ing the red sun Ris - es warm and bright; But the ev -'ning com - eth on,

And the dark cold night: There's a bright land far a - way, Where 'tis nev - er - end - ing day.

182 MORDEN.   7.5.7.5., Dble.   E. PROUT.

Fa - ther, here we ded - i - cate This new year to Thee, In what - ev - er

world - ly state Thou wilt have us be, Not from sor - row, pain, or care,

Free-dom dare we claim; This a - lone shall be our prayer: "Glo - ri - fy Thy name."

183 AT THE CROSS THERE'S ROOM. 7.5.7.5.7.7.7.5. REV. R. LOWRY.

Mourn - er, where - so - e'er thou art, At the cross there's room! Tell the bur - den

of thy heart: At the cross there's room! Tell it in thy Sa-viour's ear, Cast a -

way thine ev - 'ry fear, On - ly speak, and He will hear; At the cross there's room!

184 THE GOLDEN RULE. 7.5.7.5.4.7.4.5.

JOHN ADCOCK.

Nev - er lose the gold - en rule, Keep it still in view;

Do to o - thers as you would They should do to you. Kind - ly, gen - tly,

In their bur - den bear a part; Meek - ly chid - ing With a lov - ing heart.

185 WORK, FOR THE NIGHT IS COMING. 7.6.7.5., Dble.

Work, for the night is com - ing, Work thro' the morn-ing hours, Work while the dew is

spark - ling, Work 'mid spring-ing flowers; Work when the day grows bright - er,

Work in the glow-ing sun; Work, for the night is com-ing, When man s work is done.

83

186 ONE MORE DAY'S WORK FOR JESUS.

7.6.5.5.6.4.6, with Chorus.

F. C. Maker.

187 ONE MORE DAY'S WORK FOR JESUS.

7.6.5.5.6.4.5., with Chorus.

F. C. Maker.

188 AUTUMN.　　　7.6.7.6.　　　MENDELSSOHN.

The dark-ness now is o-ver, And all the world is bright;

Praise be to Christ who keep-eth His chil-dren safe at night!

189 BARTON.　　　7.6.7.6.　　　J. H. KNECHT.

O hap-py band of pil-grims, If on-ward ye will tread,

With Je-sus as your Fel-low, To Je-sus as your Head!

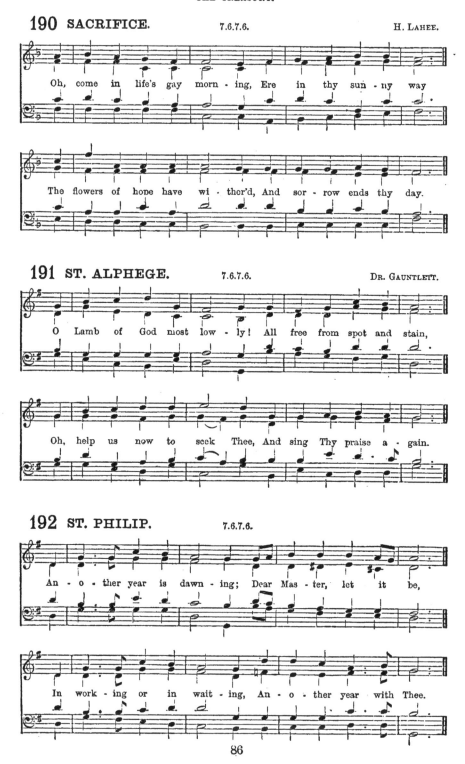

190 SACRIFICE.   7.6.7.6.   H. Lahee.

Oh, come in life's gay morn - ing, Ere in thy sun - ny way

The flowers of hope have wi - ther'd, And sor - row ends thy day.

191 ST. ALPHEGE.   7.6.7.6.   Dr. Gauntlett.

O Lamb of God most low - ly! All free from spot and stain,

Oh, help us now to seek Thee, And sing Thy praise a - gain.

192 ST. PHILIP.   7.6.7.6.

An - o - ther year is dawn - ing; Dear Mas - ter, let it be,

In work - ing or in wait - ing, An - o - ther year with Thee.

193 JESUS, KEEP ME.   7.6.7.6.6.6.7.6.   W. H. DOANE.

Je - sus, keep me near the cross! There a pre-cious foun - tain, Free to all — a

heal-ing stream —Flows from Cal - v'ry's moun - tain.   In the cross, In the cross

Be my glo - ry ev - er, Till my raptured soul shall find Rest be-yond the riv - er.

194 PILGRIMAGE.   7.6.7.6.7.6.7.3.   T. L. SELBY. From the "School Hymnal Tune Book."

The world looks ve - ry beau-ti - ful And full of joy to me; The sun shines out in

glo - ry On ev - 'ry-thing I see; I know I shall be hap-py While

in the world I stay, For I will fol - low Je - sus— All the way.

195 ANGELS' STORY. * 8 lines, 7.6.

DR. A. H. MANN.

I love to hear the sto - ry Which an - gel voi - ces tell, How once the King of

glo - ry Came down on earth to dwell. I am both weak and sin - ful, But

this I sure - ly know, The Lord came down to save me Be - cause He loved me so.

196 AURELIA.

8 lines, 7.6.   DR. WESLEY. From DR. S. S. WESLEY'S "European Psalmist," by per.

An - o - ther Sab - bath end - ed, Its peace-ful hours all flown, We come to close its

wor - ship, O Lord, be - fore Thy throne. We bless Thee for this earn - est Of

bet - ter rest a - bove; This to - ken of Thy kind-ness, This pledge of boundless love.

197 "COME UNTO ME." 8 lines, 7.6. Rev. J. B. Dykes, Mus. Doc. From "Hymns Ancient and Modern," by per.

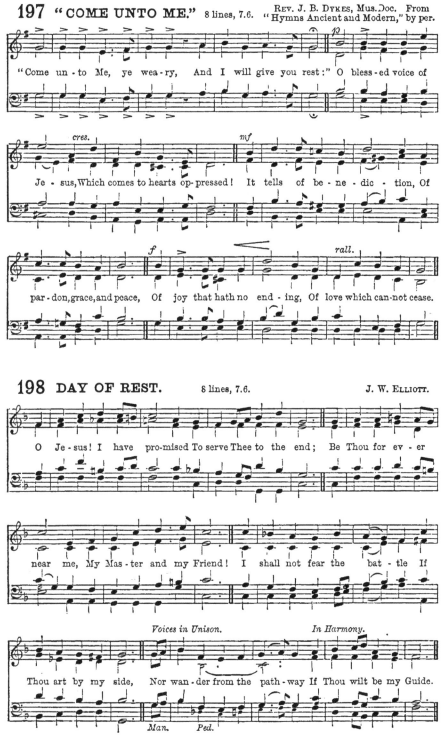

"Come un-to Me, ye wea-ry, And I will give you rest:" O bless-ed voice of Je-sus, Which comes to hearts op-pressed! It tells of be-ne-dic-tion, Of par-don, grace, and peace, Of joy that hath no end-ing, Of love which can-not cease.

198 DAY OF REST. 8 lines, 7.6. J. W. Elliott.

O Je-sus! I have pro-mised To serve Thee to the end; Be Thou for ev-er near me, My Mas-ter and my Friend! I shall not fear the bat-tle If Thou art by my side, Nor wan-der from the path-way If Thou wilt be my Guide.

Voices in Unison. *In Harmony.*

Man. Ped.

199. DEDHAM. * 8 lines, 7.6, Arr. ANDREW DEAKIN.
From HAYDN.

Go when the morn-ing shin-eth, Go when the noon is bright, Go when the eve de-
- -clin-eth, Go in the hush of night; Go with pure mind and feel-ing, Fling
ev - 'ry fear a - way, And in thy cham-ber kneel-ing, Do thou in se - cret pray.

200 DUNKIRK. 8 lines, 7.6.

When, His sal - va - tion bring - ing, To Zi - on Je - sus came, The
child - ren all stood sing - ing Ho - san - na to His name; Nor
did their zeal of - fend Him, But as He rode a - long He

201 HARLINGTON. 8 lines, 7.6. M. HAYDN.

let them still at - tend Him, He let them still at - tend Him, He

let them still at - tend Him, Well pleased to hear their song.

O Thou, whose hand has brought us Un - to this joy - ful day,

Ac - cept our glad thanks - giv - ing, And lis - ten as we pray;

And may our pre - pa - ra - tion For this day's ser - vice be......

With one ac - cord to of - - fer Our - selves, O Lord, to Thee.

202 EWING.   8 lines, 7.6.   BISHOP OF ARGYLL.

Je - ru - sa - lem the gold - en, With milk and ho - ney blest! Be - neath thy con - tem-

- pla - tion, Sink heart and voice op - prest. I know not, oh, I know not What

joys a - wait us there; What ra - dian - cy of glo - ry, What bliss be - yond com - pare!

203 GREENLAND.   8 lines, 7.6.   From "Psalms and Hymns for Divine Worship," by per.

Come, let us sing of Je - sus, While hearts and ac - cents blend; Come, let us sing of

Je - sus, The sin - ner's on - ly Friend: His ho - ly soul re - joi - ces, A -

- mid the choirs a - bove, To hear our youth-ful voi - ces Ex - ult - ing in His love.

204 HEBER. *   8 lines, 7.6.   Ascribed to BISHOP HEBER

From Greenland's i - cy moun-tains, From In-dia's cor - al strand, Where Af-ric's sun - ny
foun - tains Roll down their gold - en sand; From many an an - cient riv - er, From
many a palm - y plain, They call us to de - liv - er Their land from er -ror's chain.

205 LYMINGTON. *   8 lines, 7.6.   ROBERT JACKSON.

Come, Christian youths and maid-ens, Come, bro-thers, old and young, Up - lift your hearts and
voi - ces, Be praise on ev - 'ry tongue. In God's own house we ga - ther, Our
year - ly feast to hold; Come, join our youth-ful an - them, Ye bro-thers, young and old.

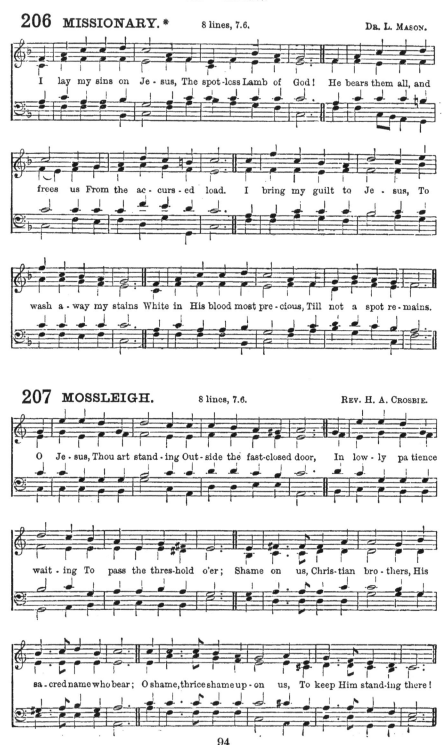

206 MISSIONARY. *   8 lines, 7.6.   DR. L. MASON.

I lay my sins on Je - sus, The spot-less Lamb of God! He bears them all, and frees us From the ac - curs - ed load. I bring my guilt to Je - sus, To wash a - way my stains White in His blood most pre - cious, Till not a spot re - mains.

207 MOSSLEIGH.   8 lines, 7.6.   REV. H. A. CROSBIE.

O Je - sus, Thou art stand - ing Out - side the fast-closed door, In low - ly pa tience wait - ing To pass the thres-hold o'er; Shame on us, Chris-tian bro - thers, His sa - cred name who bear; O shame, thrice shame up - on us, To keep Him stand-ing there!

208 MUNICH. * 8 lines, 7.6. German.

O Je-sus! meek and low - ly, Who once did so-journ here; O Je-sus! pure and ho - ly, Thy gen - tle voice I hear! It speaks from out the pa - ges Of Thine own Book di - vine; It comes all down the a - ges, To wea-ry hearts like mine.

209 NEW YORK. * 8 lines, 7.6. G. J. WEBB.

Hail to the Lord's A - noint - ed, Great Da-vid's great-er Son! Hail, in the time ap - point - ed, His reign on earth be - gun! He comes to break op - pres - sion, To set the cap-tive free; To take a-way trans-gres-sion, And rule in e - qui - ty.

95

210 ST. GEORGE'S, BOLTON. 8 lines, 7.6. J. WALCH.

I need Thee, pre-cious Je - sus! For I am full of sin; My soul is dark and guil - ty, My heart is dead with - in; I need the cleansing foun-tain, Where I can al - ways flee, The blood of Christ most pre-cious, The sin-ner's per - fect plea.

211 ST. THEODULPH. * 8 lines, 7.6. MELCHIOR TESCHNER.

Lord of the liv - ing har - vest, That whi-tens o'er the plain, Where an - gels soon shall ga - ther Their sheaves of gold - en grain; Ac - cept these hands to la - bour, These hearts to trust and love, And deign with them to hast - en Thy kingdom from a - bove.

212 SCHUBERT. 8 lines, 7.6. SCHUBERT. From the "School Hymnal Tune Book."

God loves the lit-tle spar-rows, And guides them as they fly, And feeds them in His kind-ness, Lest they should faint and die; He teach-es them their mu-sic, That they may tell His praise, A-mong the wav-ing branch-es, In sum-mer's gold-en days.

213 SHILOH (ENDSLEIGH). * 8 lines, 7.6. S. SALVATORI. By per. of J. NISBET & Co.

O day of rest and glad-ness, O day of joy and light, O balm of care and sad-ness, Most beau-ti-ful, most bright; On thee the high and low-ly, Be-fore th'e-ter-nal throne, Sing Ho-ly, Ho-ly, Ho-ly, To the great Three in One!

214 **BENIGNUS.** 8 lines, 7.6., with Chorus. DR. A. S. HOLLOWAY.

I love to tell the Sto - ry, Of un - seen things a - bove, Of

Je - sus and His glo - ry, Of Je - sus and His love! I love to tell the

Sto - ry, Be - cause I know it's true; It sa - tis - fies my long - ing, As

CHORUS.

no - thing else would do. I love to tell the Sto - ry! 'Twill be my theme in

glo - ry, To tell the Old, Old Sto - ry, Of Je - sus and His love.

215 **I LOVE TO TELL THE STORY.** *

8 lines, 7.6., with Chorus. W. G. FISCHER.

I love to tell the Sto - ry, Of un - seen things a - bove, Of

Je - sus and His glo - ry, Of Je - sus and His love! I love to tell the

Sto - ry, Be - cause I know it's true; It sa - tis - fies my long - ing, As

CHORUS.

no - thing else would do. I love to tell the Sto - ry! 'Twill be my theme in

glo - ry, To tell the Old, Old Sto - ry, Of Je - sus and His love.

216 ST. ALPHEGE. 7.6.8.6. DR. GAUNTLETT.

I want to be like Je - sus, So low - ly and so meek,

For no one marked an an - gry word, That ev - er heard Him speak.

99

217 I LOVE THE NAME OF JESUS.

8 lines, 7.6., with Chorus.

By permission of
the Sunday School Union

I love the name of Je - sus, The name the an - gels sing;

And with their loud ho - san - nas The heaven - ly por - tals ring:

To Him my all - con - fid - ing, In Him my joy com - plete,

I learn, with Chris - tian meek - ness, My du - ty at His feet.

CHORUS.

I love,...... I love,...... I love the name of Je - sus, The

I love, I love,

sweet - est name, the name,...... The name the an - gels sing.

the sweet - est name.

218 TELL ME THE OLD, OLD STORY.

8 lines, 7.6., with Chorus.

W. H. DOANE.

Tell me the Old, Old Story, Of un-seen things a-bove,

Of Je-sus and His glo-ry, Of Je-sus and His love:

Tell me the Sto-ry sim-ply, As to a lit-tle child,

For I am weak and wea-ry, And help-less and de-filed.

CHORUS.

Tell me the Old, Old Sto-ry, Tell me the Old, Old Sto-ry,

Tell me the Old, Old Sto-ry, Of Je-sus and His love.

219 SAFE IN THE ARMS OF JESUS.

8 lines, 7.6., with Chorus.

W. H. DOANE.

Safe in the arms of Je - sus, Safe on His gen - tle breast,

rit.　　　　　　　　　*End.*

There by His love o'er - shad - ed, Sweet - ly my soul shall rest.

Hark ! 'tis the voice of An - gels Borne in a song to me,

D.C. CHORUS.

O - ver the fields of glo - ry, O - ver the jas - per sea........

220 WE PLOUGH THE FIELDS.

8 lines, 7.6., with Refrain.

J. A. E. SCHULTZE.

We plough the fields, and scat - ter The good seed on the land, But it is fed and

wa - tered By God's al - migh - ty hand ; He sends the snow in win - ter, The

102

warmth to swell the grain, The breez-es, and the sun-shine, And soft re-fresh-ing rain.

REFRAIN.

All good gifts a - round us Are sent from heaven a - bove,

Then thank the Lord, O thank the Lord, For all........ His love!

221 FOLLOW ME. 7.6.7.6.7.7.7.6. German. From the "School Hymnal Tune Book," by permission.

SOLO. CHORUS. SOLO.

"Fol-low Me," the Mas-ter said: We will fol-low Je - sus; By His word and

CHORUS.

Spi - rit led, We will fol-low Je - sus. Still for us He lives to plead,

At the throne doth in-ter-cede, Of-fers help in time of need: We will fol-low Je - sus.

222 NEWARK.   12 lines, 7.6.   S. REAY. From the "School Hymnal Tune Book."

I love to hear the sto - ry Which an - gel voi - ces tell,

How once the King of glo - ry Came down on earth to dwell.

I am both weak and sin - ful, But this I sure - ly know.

The Lord came down to save me, Be - cause He loved me so.

I love to hear the sto - ry Which an - gel voi - ces tell,

How once the King of glo - ry Came down on earth to dwell.

223 HOW MANY SHEEP ARE STRAYING.

8 lines, 7.6., with Chorus.

R. LOWRY.

How ma - ny sheep are stray - ing, Lost from the Sa - viour's fold!

Up - on the lone - ly moun - tain They shiv - er with the cold;

With - in the tan - gled thick - ets Where poi - son - vines do creep,

And o - ver rock - y ledg - es Wan - der the poor lost sheep.

CHORUS.

Oh, come, let us go and find them! In the paths of death they roam; At the

close of the day, 'twill be sweet to say, "I have brought some lost one home."

224 SING WITH A TUNEFUL SPIRIT.

7.6.7.6.7.6.8.6.

W. F. SHERWIN.

Sing with a tune-ful spi - rit, Sing with a cheer-ful lay, Praise to thy great Cre-

-a - tor; While on the pil-grim way. Sing when the birds are wak - ing,

Sing with the morning light, Sing in the noontide's golden beam, Sing in the hush of night.

225 ST. ANATOLIUS. 7.6.7.6.8.8.

A. H. BROWN.

The day is past and o - ver; All thanks, O Lord, to Thee !

We pray Thee now that sin - less The hours of dark may be;

O Je - sus, keep us in Thy sight, And guard us thro' the com - ing night!

226 BELLEVUE. 7:6.8.6.7.6.8.6. W. C. FILBY.

Ten thou-sand times ten thou-sand, In spark-ling rai-ment bright, The ar-mies of the ransomed saints Throng up the steeps of light: 'Tis fin-ished! all is fin-ished,Their fight with death and sin; Fling o-pen wide the gold-en gates And let the vic-tors in.

227 TREVU. 7.6.8.6.8.6.8.6. H. A. SMITH, M.A. From the "Methodist Sunday School Tune Book," by per.

We won't give up the Sab-bath, The day which God hath blessed, That all the wea-ry sons of toil Might taste of heaven-ly rest; The day of joy, and praise, and prayer, The bright-est of the seven, When, loosed from ev-'ry earth-ly care, We think of God and heaven.

107

228 WICLIF. 7.6.8.6.8.6.8.6., with Chorus. T. S. GUEST.

We won't give up the Bi - ble, God's ho - ly book of truth;

The bless - ed staff of hoa - ry age, The guide of ear - ly youth;

The sun that sheds a glo - rious light O'er ev - 'ry drea - ry road;

The voice that speaks a Sa - viour's love, And calls us home to God. We

won't give up the Bi - ble, God's ho - ly book of truth; The bless - ed staff of

hoa - ry age, The guide of ear - ly youth, The guide of ear - ly youth.

229 BENEATH THE CROSS OF JESUS.

7.6.8.6.8.6.8.6.

IRA D. SANKEY.

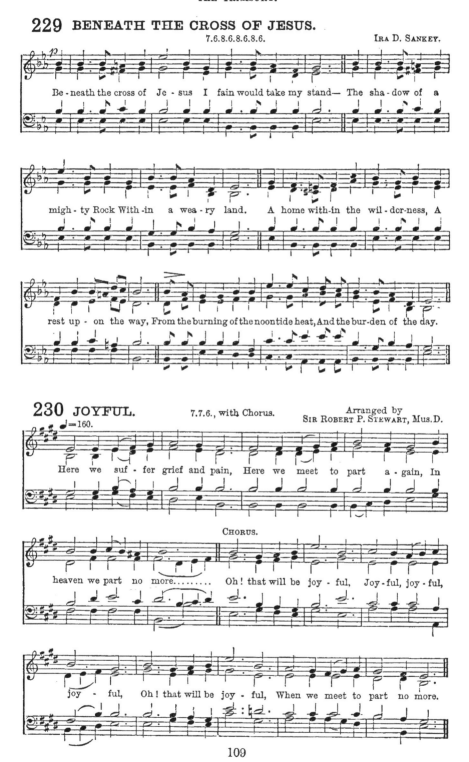

Be-neath the cross of Je - sus I fain would take my stand— The sha - dow of a migh - ty Rock With -in a wea - ry land. A home with-in the wil - der-ness, A rest up - on the way, From the burning of the noontide heat, And the bur-den of the day.

230 JOYFUL.

7.7.6., with Chorus.

Arranged by
SIR ROBERT P. STEWART, Mus. D.

♩ = 160.

Here we suf - fer grief and pain, Here we meet to part a - gain, In

CHORUS.

heaven we part no more........ Oh! that will be joy - ful, Joy-ful, joy - ful, joy - ful, Oh! that will be joy - ful, When we meet to part no more.

231 LACRYMÆ.   7.7.7.   Dr. A. Sullivan.

Je - sus, to Thy ta - ble led, Now let ev - 'ry

heart be fed With the true and liv - ing Bread.

232 VIGILATE.   7.7.7.3.   Dr. W. H. Monk. From "Hymns Ancient and Modern," by per.

"Chris - tian! seek not yet re - pose," Hear thy guar - dian An - gel say;

Thou art in the midst of foes; "Watch......... and pray."

233 CAPETOWN. *   7.7.7.5.   Dr. Filitz.

Ev - er bless - ed Tri - ni - ty, Source of life and pu - ri - ty,

Hear us, while we lift to Thee Ho - ly chant and psalm.

234 WANSWELL. * 7.7.7.5. Jos. Bennett.
From ' Congregational Church Music."

Fear - less, calm, and strong in love, Wouldst thou ply the Gos - pel net?

Then re - mem - ber God a - bove, And thy - self for - get.

235 CHESTER. 7.7.7.7. A. Stone.

Take my life, and let it be Con - se - crat - ed, Lord, to Thee!

Take my mo - ments and my days, Let them flow in cease - less praise.

236 DIJON. 7.7.7.7. German Evening Hymn.

Soft - ly fades the twi - light ray Of the ho - ly Sab - bath - day;

Gen - tly as life's set - ting sun When the Chris - tian's course is run.

237 ELLINGHAM. 7.7.7.7. REV. S. N. GODFREY.

Let us sing with one ac-cord Praise to Je-sus Christ our Lord;

He is wor-thy whom we praise; Hearts and voi-ces let us raise.

238 GERMAN HYMN. * 7.7.7.7. PLEYEL. Arranged by W. C. FILBY.

God of mer-cy, throned on high, Lis-ten from Thy lof-ty seat;

Hear, O hear our fee-ble cry; Guide, O guide our wan-d'ring feet.

239 HART'S. * 7.7.7.7. MILGROVE. Arranged by W. C. FILBY.

Gen-tle Je-sus, meek and mild, Look up-on a lit-tle child;

Pi-ty my sim-pli-ci-ty, Teach me, Lord, to come to Thee.

240 INNOCENTS. * 7.7.7.7.

Let us with a glad-some mind Praise the Lord, for He is kind:

For His mer-cies shall en-dure, Ev-er faith-ful, ev-er sure.

241 KIEL. 7.7.7.7. From ROMBERG.

Je-sus, Lord of Sab-bath rest, Waft Thy Sab-bath o'er my breast,

Let the ev-'ning bless-ing come, Soft and still as thoughts of home.

242 NOTTINGHAM. 7.7.7.7. From MOZART.

Je-sus, Sa-viour, Bro-ther, Lord! All our ful-ness is in Thee;

All our joy shall ev-er be On to press to Thine a-bode!

243 PERCY.   7.7.7.7.   JOHN ADCOCK.

Bless - ed Je - sus, life is fair, I have known no se - cret care;

Sun - beams all a - round me rest, Joy is still my bo - som's guest.

244 PULCHRA.   7.7.7.7   ROBERT HOWARTH. From MAJOR'S "Tunes and Chants for Home and School."

Soon shall set the Sab - bath sun; Soon the sa - cred day be done;

But a sweet - er rest re - mains Where the glo - rious Sa - viour reigns.

245 REDHEAD. *   7.7.7.7.   R. REDHEAD.

Ho - ly Fa - ther, hear my cry; Ho - ly Sa - viour, bend Thine ear;

Ho - ly Spi - rit, come Thou nigh: Fa - ther, Sa - viour, Spi - rit, hear!

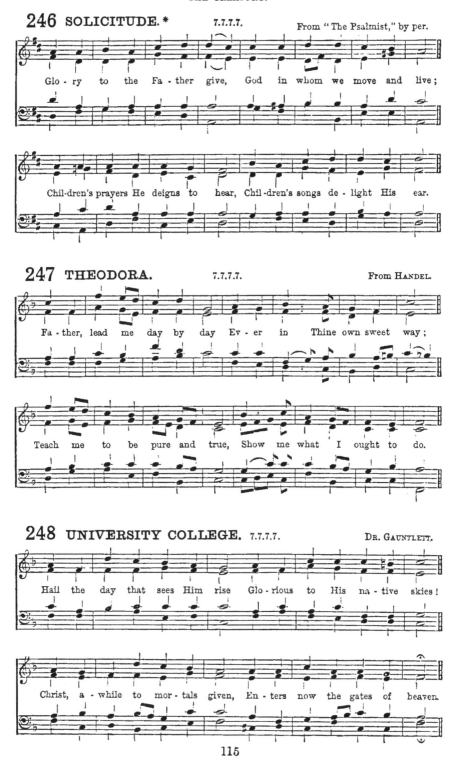

246 SOLICITUDE. *   7.7.7.7.   From "The Psalmist," by per.

Glo - ry to the Fa - ther give, God in whom we move and live;

Chil-dren's prayers He deigns to hear, Chil-dren's songs de - light His ear.

247 THEODORA.   7.7.7.7.   From HANDEL.

Fa - ther, lead me day by day Ev - er in Thine own sweet way;

Teach me to be pure and true, Show me what I ought to do.

248 UNIVERSITY COLLEGE. 7.7.7.7.   DR. GAUNTLETT.

Hail the day that sees Him rise Glo - rious to His na - tive skies!

Christ, a - while to mor - tals given, En - ters now the gates of heaven.

249 CHILDREN OF JERUSALEM.
7.7.7.7., with Refrain.

Air from the "Methodist Sunday School Tune Book," by per.

Chil - dren of Je - ru - sa - lem Sang the praise of Je - sus' name;

Chil - dren, too, of la - ter days Join to sing the Sa - viour's praise.

REFRAIN.

Hark, hark, hark! while youth - ful voi - ces sing, Hark, hark,

hark! while youth - ful voi - ces sing Loud ho - san - nas,

loud ho - san - nas, loud ho - san - nas to our King.

250 EASTER HYMN. * 7.7.7.7., with Hallelujah.

H. CAREY.

"Christ, the Lord, is risen to - day!" Hal - - - le - lu - jah!
"Christ, the Lord, is risen to - day!" Sons of men and an - gels say;

116

Sons of men and an - gels say; Hal - - - le - lu - jah!
Raise your joy and tri - umph high, Sing, ye heavens, and earth, re - ply!

Raise your joy and tri - umph high, Hal - - - le - lu - jah!
Love's re - deem - ing work is done; Fought the fight, the bat - tle won:

Sing, ye heavens, and earth, re - ply! Hal - - - le - lu - jah!
Lo! our Sun's e - clipse is o'er; Lo! He sets in blood no more.

May also be sung as 8 lines, 7s., as shewn in *italics*.

251 HAVERSTOCK.*   7.7.7.7.7.   J. NEANDER.

Hal - le - lu - jah! Praise the Lord! Praise Him for His faith - ful Word; For the

peace of pard'ning love, Praise His name, all names a - bove. Hal - le - lu-jah! Praise the Lord!

252 JESUS LOVES ME. 7.7.7.7.5.5.5.6.   W. B. BRADBURY.

Je - sus loves me! this I know, For the Bi - ble tells me so; Lit - tle ones to

Him be - long, They are weak, but He is strong. Yes, Je - sus loves me,

Yes, Je - sus loves me, Yes, Je - sus loves me, The Bi - ble tells me so.

253 CASSEL. *   6 lines, 7s. "Choral Book of the Bohemian Brethren."

Hark! a still small voice is heard Gen - tly speak - ing from a - bove:

'Tis the great Re - deem - er's word, 'Tis the mes - sage of His love.

Hear the call to you ad - dressed, Ye who would be tru - ly blessed.

118

254 DIX.   6 lines, 7s.   CONRAD KOCHER.

As with glad-ness men of old Did the guid-ing star be-hold:

As with joy they hailed its light, Lead-ing on-ward, beam-ing bright!

So, most gra-cious Lord, may we Ev-er-more be led to Thee.

255 NASSAU.   6 lines, 7s.   J. ROSENMULLER.

For the beau-ty of the earth, For the beau-ty of the skies,

For the love which from our birth O-ver and a-round us lies:

Christ, our God, to Thee we raise This, our sa-cri-fice of praise.

256 EGLON. 6 lines, 7s. MORETON. By permission of the Sunday School Union.

Saved our-selves by Je-sus' blood, Let us now draw

near to God, Let us now.... draw near to God.

Ma-ny round us blind-ly stray: Moved with pi-ty,

let us pray— Pray that they who now are blind Soon the way of

peace may find, Soon.... the way........ of peace may find.

257 MORNING STAR. 6 lines, 7s. From HAYDN. By permission of MR. CURWEN.

All things praise Thee— Lord most high, Heaven and earth, and

sea, and sky; All were for Thy glo - ry made,

That Thy great - ness, thus dis - played, Should all wor - ship

bring to Thee; All things praise Thee: Lord, may we?

258 REQUIEM.   6 lines, 7s.   W. SCHULTHES.

Lo! at noon, 'tis sud - den night, Dark - ness co - vers all the sky;

Rocks are rend - ing at the sight; Chil - dren, can you tell me why?

What can all these won - ders be? Je - sus died on Cal - va - ry.

Org.

259 SPAIN. *   6 lines, 7s.   Arranged by Dr. ARTHUR S. HOLLOWAY.

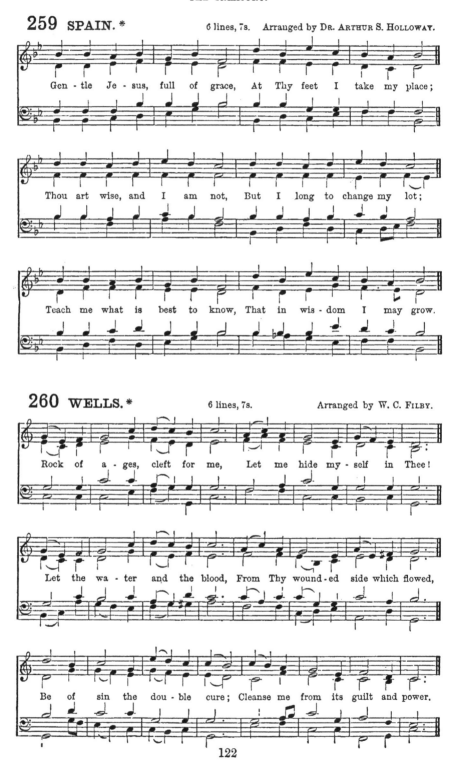

Gen - tle Je - sus, full of grace, At Thy feet I take my place;

Thou art wise, and I am not, But I long to change my lot;

Teach me what is best to know, That in wis - dom I may grow.

260 WELLS. *   6 lines, 7s.   Arranged by W. C. FILBY.

Rock of a - ges, cleft for me, Let me hide my - self in Thee!

Let the wa - ter and the blood, From Thy wound - ed side which flowed,

Be of sin the dou - ble cure; Cleanse me from its guilt and power.

261 **BENEVENTO.**   8 lines, 7s.   From S. WEBBE, Senr.

Lord, from whom all bless-ings flow, Per-fect-ing the Church be - low, Stead-fast may we

cleave to Thee; Love the my-stic un-ion be. Join our faith-ful spi-rits, join Each to

each, and all to Thine; Lead us thro' the paths of peace, On to per-fect ho-li-ness.

262 **HOLLINGSIDE.**   8 lines, 7s.   REV. J. B. DYKES, Mus.Doc. From "Hymns Ancient and Modern," by per.

Je-sus! Lov-er of my soul, Let me to Thy bo-som fly, While the rag-ing

wa-ters roll, While the tem-pest still is high: Hide me, O my Sa-viour, hide,

Till the storm of life is past; Safe in-to the ha-ven guide: Oh, receive my soul at last!

263 CHRISTMAS HYMN. * 8 lines, 7s., with Chorus.   MENDELSSOHN.

Hark! the he-rald an-gels sing Glo-ry to the new-born King,

Peace on earth, and mer-cy mild, God and sin-ners re-con-ciled!

Joy-ful, all ye na-tions, rise. Join the tri-umph of the skies;

With th'an-ge-lic host pro-claim Christ is born in Beth-le-hem!

Hark! the he-rald an-gels sing Glo-ry to the new-born King!

Org. ped.

264 IONA.   8 lines, 7s.   From COSTA'S " Eli."

God of glo-ry, God of grace, Hear from heaven, Thy dwell-ing-place,

While our fee - ble voi - ces sing Grate - ful prais - es to our King:

While we meet at Thy com - mand, Ask - ing bless-ings from Thy hand,

God of glo - ry, God of grace, Hear from heaven, Thy dwell - ing - place.

265 HONIDON.

8 lines, 7s.

REV. T. R. MATTHEWS.

Depth of mer - cy! can there be Mer - cy still re - served for me? Can my God His

wrath for-bear? Me, the chief of sin-ners, spare? I have long with-stood His grace, Long pro-voked Him

to His face; Would not heark-en to His calls, Grieved Him by a thou-sand falls.

266 ST. GEORGE'S, WINDSOR. 8 lines, 7s., Sir G. J. Elvey.

Come, ye thank-ful peo-ple, come, Raise the song of Har-vest-Home. All is safe-ly gathered in, Ere the win-ter storms be-gin; God, our Ma-ker, doth pro-vide For our wants to be sup-plied: Come to God's own tem-ple, come, Raise the song of Har-vest-Home.

267 SYRIA. * 8 lines, 7s.

Lit-tle trav-'llers Zi-on-ward, Each one en-t'ring in-to rest, In the king-dom of your Lord, In the man-sions of the blest: There, to wel-come, Je-sus waits, Gives the crown His follow'rs win; Lift your heads, ye golden gates, Let the lit-tle trav'llers in!

268 BEAUTIFUL HOME OF THE BLEST.

7.8.7.6.9.9.9.6., with Chorus.   ERNEST J. MEAD.
Partly adapted from the American.

Beau - ti - ful home of the blest, Beau - ti - ful home! beau - ti - ful home!

Home where the wea - ry ones rest, Beau - ti - ful home on high!

Home where the pure and the good shall stand, Clad in white rai-ment at God's right hand,

Cir - cling His throne in a ra - diant band, Sing - ing for ev - er there.

Beau - ti - ful home of the blest, Beau - ti - ful home on high!

Home where the wea - ry ones rest, Beau - ti - ful home on high!

269 NOCTURN. 10 lines, 7s. Arr. from COSTA's "Eli," by permission of REV. W. MERCER.

Fa-ther, by Thy love and power, Comes a-gain the ev-ning hour;

Light has van-ished, la-bours cease, Wea-ry crea-tures rest in peace:

Thou, whose ge-nial dews dis-til On the low-liest weed that grows,

Fa-ther, guard our couch from ill, Grant Thy chil-dren sweet re-pose;

We to Thee our-selves re-sign, Let our la-test thoughts be Thine.

270 SHADOWS. 7.7.7.7.8.5.8.5. DR. W. H. MONK. From the "Congregational Psalmist," by per.

Fa-ther, while the sha-dows fall With the twi-light o-ver all,

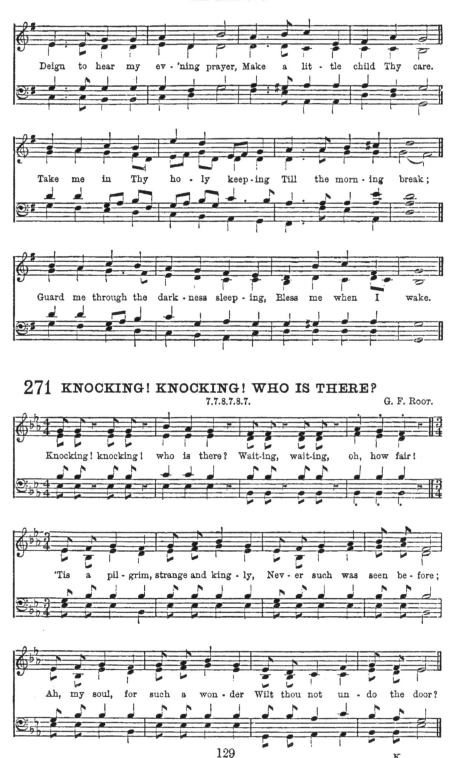

Deign to hear my ev - 'ning prayer, Make a lit - tle child Thy care.

Take me in Thy ho - ly keep-ing Till the morn - ing break;

Guard me through the dark - ness sleep - ing, Bless me when I wake.

271 KNOCKING! KNOCKING! WHO IS THERE?
7.7.8.7.8.7.

G. F. Root.

Knocking! knocking! who is there? Wait-ing, wait-ing, oh, how fair!

'Tis a pil - grim, strange and king - ly, Nev - er such was seen be - fore;

Ah, my soul, for such a won - der Wilt thou not un - do the door?

272 I AM JESUS' LITTLE FRIEND.

7.7.8.8.7.7., with Refrain.

W. H. DOANE.

I am Je-sus lit-tle friend; On His mer-cy I de-pend; If I try to please Him ev-er, If I grieve His spi-rit nev-er, Oh, how ve-ry good to me

REFRAIN.

Will my Sa-viour al-ways be! I am Je-sus' lit-tle friend; On His mer-cy I de-pend.

273 TROMSO.

7.7.8.8.7.7.

Danish Melody.

I am Je-sus' lit-tle lamb; Ev-er glad at heart I am; Je-sus loves me, Je-sus knows me, All things fair and good He shows me, E-ven calls me by my name: Ev-'ry day He is the same.

274 COME, LET US ALL UNITE. 8.3.8.3.8 8 8.3.

Come, let us all u - nite and sing, God is love! God is love!

While heaven and earth their prais - es bring: God is love! God is love!

Let ev - 'ry soul from sin a - wake, Each in his heart sweet mu - sic make,

And sweet - ly sing for Je - sus' sake: God is love! God is love!

275 BROOKFIELD. 8.5.8.3. G. B. THACKWRAY.

Lord, I read of ten - der mer - cy In Thy life on earth;

An - gels sang of peace and good - ness At Thy birth.

276 TABOR. 8.3.8.3.8.8.8.3.

There is a bet - ter world, they say, Oh, so bright! Oh, so bright!

Where sin and woe are done a - way, Oh, so bright! Oh, so bright!

And mu - sic fills the balm - y air, And an - gels bright and

pure are there, And harps of gold and man-sions fair, Oh, so bright! Oh, so bright!

277 JESUS LITTLE CHILDREN BLESSES. From MAJOR'S "Tunes and Chants for Home and School."
8.4.8.4.8.8.8.4.

Je - sus lit - tle chil - dren bless - es: Oh! how He loves!

Fond - ly He each lamb ca - ress - es: Oh! how He loves!

132

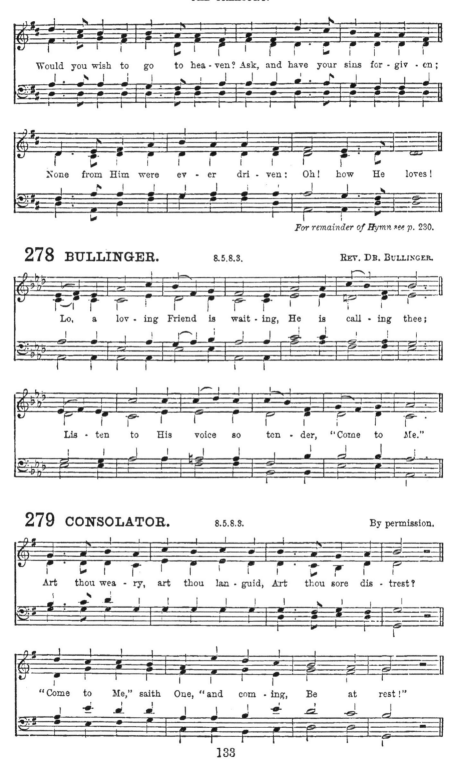

Would you wish to go to hea - ven? Ask, and have your sins for - giv - en;

None from Him were ev - er dri - ven: Oh! how He loves!

For remainder of Hymn see p. 230.

278 BULLINGER.   8.5.8.3.   REV. DR. BULLINGER.

Lo, a lov - ing Friend is wait - ing, He is call - ing thee;

Lis - ten to His voice so ten - der, "Come to Me."

279 CONSOLATOR.   8.5.8.3.   By permission.

Art thou wea - ry, art thou lan - guid, Art thou sore dis - trest?

"Come to Me," saith One, "and com - ing, Be at rest!"

280 STEPHANOS. 8.5.8.3. REV. SIR H. W. BAKER. From "Hymns Ancient and Modern," by per.

Art thou wea - ry, art thou lan - guid, Art thou sore dis - trest?

"Come to Me," saith One, "and, com - ing, Be at rest!"

281 ANGEL VOICES EVER SINGING. 8.5.8.5.8.4.3. DR. A. SULLIVAN.

An - gel voi - ces ev - er sing - ing Round Thy throne of light;

An - gel harps for ev - er ring - ing, Rest not day nor night:

Thou-sands on - ly live to bless Thee, And con - fess Thee, Lord of might.

282 PASS ME NOT. 8.5.8.5., with Chorus. W. H. DOANE.

Pass me not, O gra cious Sa - viour, Hear my hum-ble cry; While on o-thers Thou art

CHORUS.

call - ing, Do not pass me by. Sa - viour, Sa - viour, Hear my hum-ble cry,

And while o - thers Thou art call - ing, Do not pass me by.

283 NEWPORT. 8.6.7.6.7.6.7.6. A. R. WATSON. From the "School Hymnal Tune Book." by per.

There's a Friend for lit - tle chil - dren, A - bove the bright blue sky;

A Friend who nev - er chang - eth, Whose love can nev - er die:

Un - like our friends by na - ture, Who change with chang - ing years,

This Friend is al - ways wor - thy The pre - cious name He bears.

284 NATIVITY.   8.6.6.8.6.6.   F. C. Maker.

All my heart this night re - joi - ces, As I hear, far and near,

Sweet - est an - gel voi - ces; "Christ is born!" their choirs are sing - ing,

Till the air, ev - 'ry - where, Now with joy is ring - ing.

285 WHEN HE COMETH.   8.6.8.5., with Chorus.   G. F. Root.

When He com-eth, when He com- eth To make up His jew - els, All His jew-els, pre-cious

Chorus.

jew - els, His loved and His own. Like the stars of the morn-ing, His

bright crown a - dorn - ing, They shall shine in their beau - ty Bright gems for His crown.

286 WREFORD. 8.6.8.4. Rev. E. S. Carter.

Our blest Re-deem-er, ere He breathed His ten-der, last fare-well,

A Guide, a Com-fort-er be-queathed With us to dwell.

287 THE SWEETEST NAME. 8.6.8.5.8.8.8.5. Arthur Page. From the "School Hymnal Tune Book," by per.

The sweet-est name in heaven a-bove, Chil-dren sing, chil-dren sing,

Our bless-ed Sa-viour crowned with love, Chil-dren sing to-day.

The Friend, whose ev-er watch-ful care Will guard our feet from ev-'ry snare,

Who loves to hear our earn-est prayer, Chil-dren sing to-day.

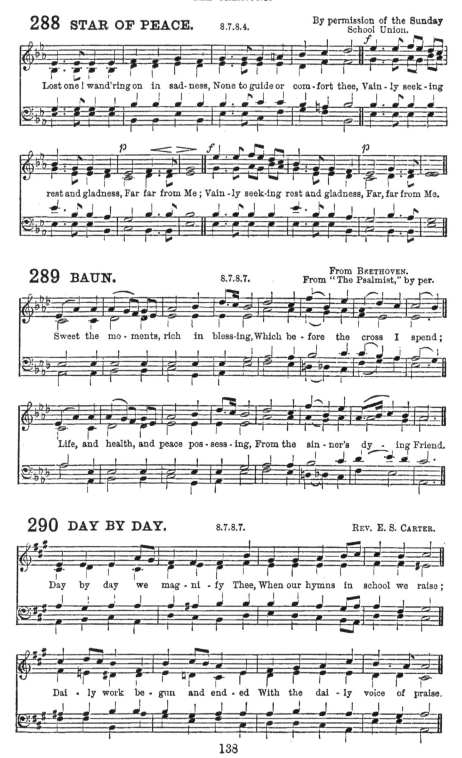

288 STAR OF PEACE. 8.7.8.4.

By permission of the Sunday School Union.

Lost one! wand'ring on in sad-ness, None to guide or com-fort thee, Vain-ly seek-ing rest and gladness, Far far from Me; Vain-ly seek-ing rest and gladness, Far, far from Me.

289 BAUN. 8.7.8.7.

From BEETHOVEN. From "The Psalmist," by per.

Sweet the mo-ments, rich in bless-ing, Which be-fore the cross I spend; Life, and health, and peace pos-sess-ing, From the sin-ner's dy-ing Friend.

290 DAY BY DAY. 8.7.8.7.

REV. E. S. CARTER.

Day by day we mag-ni-fy Thee, When our hymns in school we raise; Dai-ly work be-gun and end-ed With the dai-ly voice of praise.

138

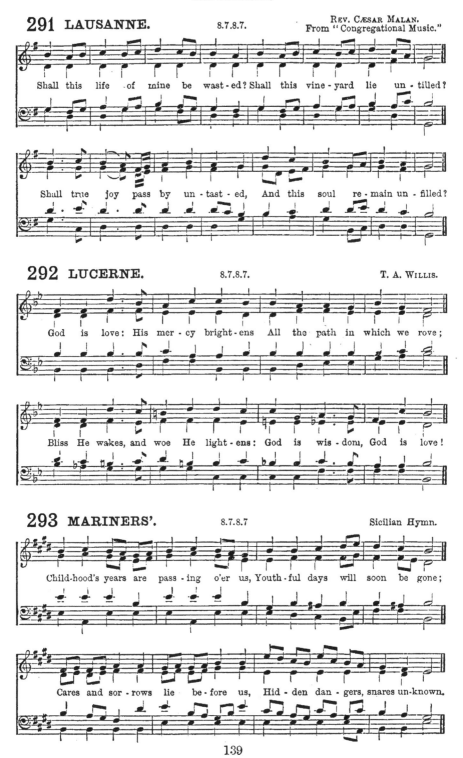

291 LAUSANNE. 8.7.8.7. REV. CÆSAR MALAN.
From "Congregational Music."

Shall this life of mine be wast-ed? Shall this vine-yard lie un-tilled?

Shall true joy pass by un-tast-ed, And this soul re-main un-filled?

292 LUCERNE. 8.7.8.7. T. A. WILLIS.

God is love: His mer-cy bright-ens All the path in which we rove;

Bliss He wakes, and woe He light-ens: God is wis-dom, God is love!

293 MARINERS'. 8.7.8.7 Sicilian Hymn.

Child-hood's years are pass-ing o'er us, Youth-ful days will soon be gone;

Cares and sor-rows lie be-fore us, Hid-den dan-gers, snares un-known.

294 ST. HELEN. 8.7.8.7

Chil - dren, join to praise the Sa - viour; Praise Him who from love came down;

Let your hearts as well as voi - ces Sing a - loud of His re - nown.

295 ST. MABYN. 8.7.8.7. A. H. BROWN.

Sa - viour, who Thy flock art feed - ing, With the Shep - herd's kind - est care,

All the fee - ble gen - tly lead - ing, While the lambs Thy bo - som share.

296 SARDIS. 8.7.8.7 From BEETHOVEN.

Hark! a thrill - ing voice is sound-ing: "Christ is nigh!" it seems to say;

"Cast a - way the dreams of dark - ness, O ye chil - dren of the day!"

297 SEFTON. 8.7.8.7. Rev. H. A. Crosbie.

Je - sus calls us o'er the tu - mult Of this world's wild, rest - less sea;

Day by day His sweet voice whis - pers, Say - ing to us, "Fol - low Me."

298 SHARON. 8.7.8.7. Dr. Boyce.

Sa - viour, while my heart is ten - der, I would yield that heart to Thee;

All my powers to Thee sur - ren - der, Thine, and on - ly Thine, to be.

299 EVEN ME. 8.7.8.7., with Refrain. W. B. Bradbury.

{ Lord, I hear of showers of bless - ing Thou art scat - t'ring full and free—
{ Showers, the thirs - ty land re - fresh - ing; Let some drop - pings fall on me—

E - ven me! e - ven me! Let some drop - pings fall on me!

141

300 BRIGHTLY BEAMS OUR FATHER'S MERCY.

8.7.8.7., with Chorus.

P. P. BLISS.

Bright - ly beams our Fa - ther's mer - cy From His light - house ev - er - more;

But to us He gives the keep - ing Of the lights a - long the shore.

CHORUS.

Let the low - er lights be burn - ing! Send a gleam a - cross the wave!

Some poor faint - ing, strug - gling sea - man You may res - cue, you may save

301 SHALL WE MEET. 8.7.8.7., with Chorus.

From "Gems of Song Music,"
by permission.

Shall we meet be - yond the riv - er Where the sur - ges cease to roll,

Where in all the bright "for ev - er" Sor - row ne'er shall press the soul?

Shall we meet, shall we meet, Shall we meet, shall we meet,

Shall we meet be - yond the riv - er, Where the sur - ges cease to roll?

302 SHALL WE GATHER AT THE RIVER?

8.7.8.7., with Chorus.

REV. R. LOWRY.

Shall we ga - ther at the riv - er, Where bright an - gel feet have trod,

With its cry - stal tide for ev - er Flow-ing by the throne of God?

CHORUS.

Yes, we'll ga - ther at the riv - er, The beau - ti - ful, the beau-ti - ful riv - er;

Ga - ther with the saints at the riv - er, That flows by the throne of God.

303 BENEDICITE.   8.7.8.7.8.7.   T. BRICHER.   By permission of the Sunday School Union.

Fa - ther, let Thy be - ne - dic - tion, Gen - tly fall - ing as the dew,

And Thy ev - er - gra - cious pre-sence, Bless us all our jour - ney through;

May we ev - er, May we ev - er Keep the end of life in view.

304 BRAYLESFORD.   8.7.8.7.8.7.   DR. GAUNTLETT.

Lead us, heaven - ly Fa - ther, lead us O'er the world's tem - pest - uous sea;

Guard us, guide us, keep us, feed us, For we have no help but Thee:

Yet pos - ses - sing Ev - 'ry bless - ing, If our God our Fa - ther be.

144

305 CALVARY. *   8.7.8.7.8.7.   STANLEY.

Yes, we part, but not for ev - er, Joy - ful hopes our bo - soms swell;

Those who love the Sa - viour, nev - er Know a long, a last fare - well:

Slow.   *a tempo.*

Bliss - ful u - ni - ons, bliss - ful u - ni - ons Lie be - yond this pass - ing vale.

306 DISMISSAL. *   8.7.8.7.8.7.

Sa - viour, round Thy foot - stool bend - ing, See our youth - ful band ap - pear;

Let Thy Spi - rit, now des - cend - ing, Our pe - ti - tions deign to hear:

Thou art will - ing, Thou art will - ing, For Thy grace is al - ways near.

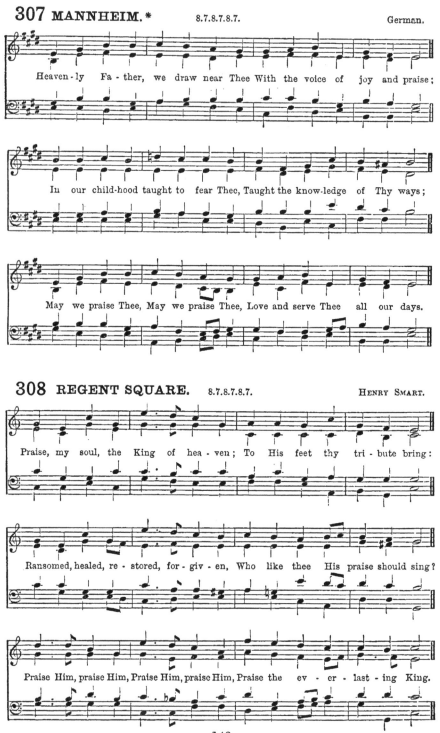

307 MANNHEIM. *   8.7.8.7.8.7.   German.

Heaven-ly Fa-ther, we draw near Thee With the voice of joy and praise;

In our child-hood taught to fear Thee, Taught the know-ledge of Thy ways;

May we praise Thee, May we praise Thee, Love and serve Thee all our days.

308 REGENT SQUARE.   8.7.8.7.8.7.   HENRY SMART.

Praise, my soul, the King of hea-ven; To His feet thy tri-bute bring:

Ransomed, healed, re-stored, for-giv-en, Who like thee His praise should sing?

Praise Him, praise Him, Praise Him, praise Him, Praise the ev-er-last-ing King.

309 ROUSSEAU. 8.7.8.7.8.7. By permission of the Sunday School Union.

Guide me, O Thou great Je - ho - vah! Pil - grim thro' this bar - ren land;

I am weak, but Thou art migh - ty, Hold me with Thy power - ful hand;

Bread of hea - ven, Bread of hea - ven, Feed me, till I want no more.

310 ST. WERBURGH. 8.7.8.7.8.7. S. WEBBE.

God Al - migh - ty, in Thy tem - ple, Low be - fore Thy throne we bow;

From Thy dwell - ing - place in glo - ry, Hear our sup - pli - ca - tions now,

While we of - fer, While we of - fer Earn - est prayer and so - lemn vow.

311 TRIUMPH. 8.7.8.7.8.7. DR. GAUNTLETT.

Glo - ry be to God the Fa - ther, Glo - ry be to God the Son,

Glo - ry be to God the Spi - rit, Great Je - ho - vah, Three in One;

Glo - ry, glo - ry, Glo - ry, glo - ry, While e - ter - nal a - ges run!

312 EVENSONG. 8.7.8.7.7.7. J. SUMMERS.

Through the day Thy love hast spared us; Now we lay us down to rest;

Through the si - lent watch - es guard us, Let no foe our peace mo - lest:

Je - sus, Thou our Guar - dian be; Sweet it is to trust in Thee.

313 GOUNOD. 8.7.8.7.7.7. C. GOUNOD.

One there is a - bove all o - thers, Well de - serves the name of Friend:

His is love be - yond a bro - ther's—Cost - ly, free, and knows no end:

They who once His kind - ness prove, Find it ev - er - last - ing love.

314 AUSTRIA. 8 lines, 8.7. F. J. HAYDN.

{ Hark, the voice of Je - sus cry - ing, Who will go and work to - day? }
{ Fields are white, and har - vests wait - ing, Who will bear the sheaves a - way? }

Loud and strong the Mas - ter call - eth, Rich re - ward He of - fers thee;

Who will an - swer, glad - ly say - ing, "Here am I, send me, send me"?

315 ANGELIC HOST. 8 lines, 8.7. W. B. BRADBURY.

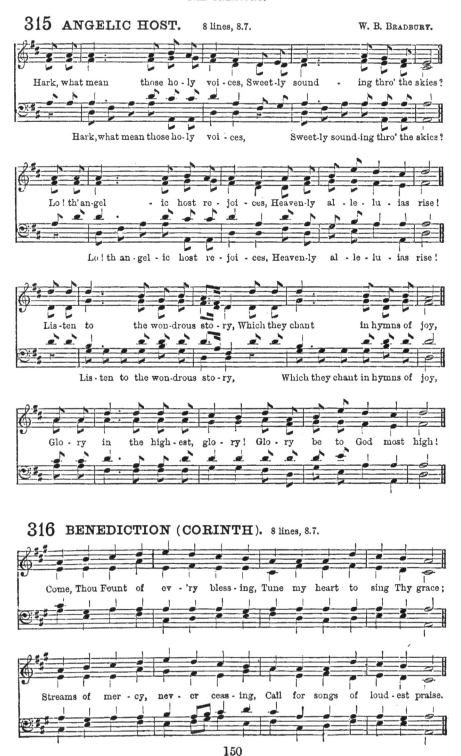

Hark, what mean those ho - ly voi - ces, Sweet-ly sound - ing thro' the skies?

Hark, what mean those ho-ly voi - ces, Sweet-ly sound-ing thro' the skies?

Lo! th'an-gel - ic host re - joi - ces, Heaven-ly al - le - lu - ias rise!

Lo! th an - gel - ic host re - joi - ces, Heaven-ly al - le - lu - ias rise!

Lis-ten to the won-drous sto - ry, Which they chant in hymns of joy,

Lis - ten to the won-drous sto - ry, Which they chant in hymns of joy,

Glo - ry in the high - est, glo - ry! Glo - ry be to God most high!

316 BENEDICTION (CORINTH). 8 lines, 8.7.

Come, Thou Fount of ev - 'ry bless - ing, Tune my heart to sing Thy grace;

Streams of mer - cy, nev - er ceas - ing, Call for songs of loud - est praise.

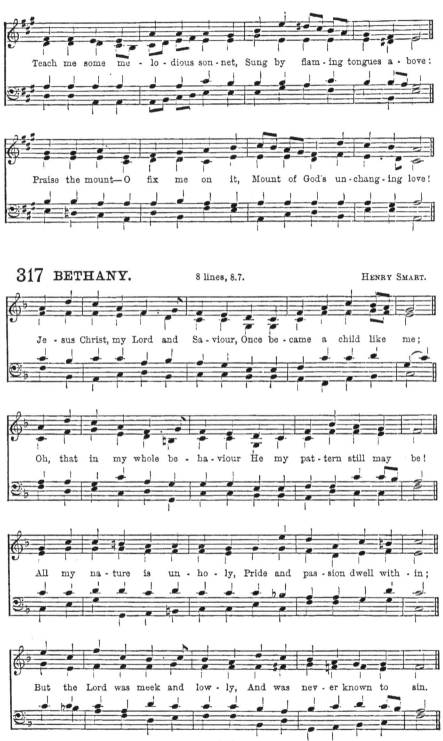

Teach me some me - lo - dious son - net, Sung by flam - ing tongues a - bove:

Praise the mount—O fix me on it, Mount of God's un - chang - ing love!

317 BETHANY.   8 lines, 8.7.   HENRY SMART.

Je - sus Christ, my Lord and Sa - viour, Once be - came a child like me;

Oh, that in my whole be - ha - viour He my pat - tern still may be!

All my na - ture is un - ho - ly, Pride and pas - sion dwell with - in;

But the Lord was meek and low - ly, And was nev - er known to sin.

318 CHICHESTER. *   8 lines, 8.7.   S. WESLEY.

Might-ty God, while an-gels bless Thee, May an in-fant sing Thy name?

Lord of men as well as an-gels, Thou art ev-'ry crea-ture's theme;

Lord of ev-'ry land and na-tion, An-cient of e-ter-nal days,

Sound-ed thro' the wide cre-a-tion Be Thy just and law-ful praise.

319 FLORENCE.   8 lines, 8.7.   Italian Melody.

Sa-viour, breathe an ev-'ning bless-ing, Ere re-pose our spi-rits seal;

Sin and want we come con-fess-ing; Thou canst save, and Thou canst heal.

Though de-struc-tion walk a-round us, Though the ar-rows past us fly,

An-gel guards from Thee sur-round us; We are safe if Thou art nigh.

320 VESPER. 8 lines, 8.7.

At Thy feet, our God and Fa-ther, Who hast blest us all our days,

We with grate-ful hearts would ga-ther, To be-gin this day with praise;—

Praise for light so bright-ly shin-ing On our steps from heaven a-bove;

Praise for mer-cies dai-ly twin-ing Round us gold-en cords of love.

321 WHAT A FRIEND. 8 lines, 8.7. C. C. CONVERSE.

What a Friend we have in Je - sus, All our sins and griefs to bear!

What a pri - vi - lege to car - ry Ev - 'ry - thing to God in prayer!

Oh, what peace we of - ten for - feit! Oh, what need - less pain we bear!

All be - cause we do not car - ry Ev - 'ry - thing to God in prayer.

322 OUR SABBATH SONG. 8.7.8.7.8.8.4.8. GEBHARDT. From the "Methodist Sunday School Tune Book." by per.

Sweet - ly dawns the Sab - bath morn - ing On the world, so full of

care; Bid - ding man for - get his la - bour, Call - ing

to the house of prayer. Oh, sweet and strong, His saints a - mong, We sing to God our Sab - bath song, Our Sab - bath song, Our Sab - bath song, We raise to Christ our Sab - bath song.

323 HEREFORD.　　　8.8.6.8.8.6.　　　Dr. Boyce.

When Thou my righ -teous Judge shalt come To fetch Thy ran - somed peo - ple home, Shall I a - mong them stand? Shall such a worth - less worm as I, Who some - times am a - fraid to die, Be found at Thy right hand?

324 CANAAN. 8 lines, 8.7., with Chorus. From "Gems of Song Music," by permission.

Oh, what has Je-sus done for me? He pi-tied me,—my Sa-viour.

My sins were great: His love was free; He died for me,—my Sa-viour.

Ex-alt-ed by the Fa-ther's side, He pleads for me,—my Sa-viour;

A heaven-ly man-sion He'll pro-vide For all who love the Sa-viour.

Je-sus, dear Je-sus, Thy name is sweet,—my Sa-viour.

When shall I see Thee face to face, My won-drous, bless-ed Sa-viour?

325 BEACON.   12 lines, 8.7.   LABAN SOLOMON. From the "School Hymnal Tune Book," by per.

O'er the wide and rest-less o - cean Of our life we speed a - long;

And to God, whose mer - cy wafts us, Will we raise our trust-ful song.

For, tho' dark the flood be - hind us, And tho' dim the track be - fore,

Yet our bark shall reach the ha - ven, On a bright and bless - ed shore.

For, at last a light shall cheer us, Soft - ly beam-ing from a - far;

And the love of Christ shall guide us Like a fade - less bea - con star.

326 WHITHER, PILGRIMS. 8.7.8.7.8.8.8.7.
W. B. BRADBURY.

Whi-ther, pil-grims, are you go-ing, Go-ing each with staff in hand?

We are go-ing on a jour-ney, Go-ing at our King's com-mand.

O-ver hills, and plains, and val-leys, We are go-ing to His pal-ace,

We are go-ing to His pal-ace, Go-ing to the bet-ter land,

We are go-ing to His pal-ace, Go-ing to the bet-ter land.

327 LISTEN, THE MASTER BESEECHETH.
8.7.9.8.8.7.9.8., with Refrain.
PHILIP PHILLIPS.

Lis-ten! the Mas-ter be-seech-eth, Call-ing each one by his name;

His voice to each lov-ing heart reach-eth, Its cheer-ful-lest ser-vice to claim.

Go where the vine-yard de-mand-eth Vine-dress-ers' nur-ture and care;

Or go where the white har-vest stand-eth, The joy of the reap-er to share.

REFRAIN.

Then work, bro-thers, work! let us slum-ber no long-er, For God's call to

la-bour grows strong-er and strong-er; The light of this life shall be

dark-ened full soon, But the light of the bet-ter life rest-eth at noon.

328 PRAISE.   8.8.6.8.8.6.   A. RADIGER.

Or two sharps. The fes - tal morn, my God, is come, That calls me
to Thy hon - oured dome, Thy pre . . . sence
to a - dore: My feet the sum - mons shall at - tend, With
will - ing steps Thy courts as - cend, And tread the hal - lowed floor,
And tread the hal - lowed floor; My feet the sum - mons shall at - tend,
With will - ing steps Thy courts as - cend, And tread the hal - lowed floor.

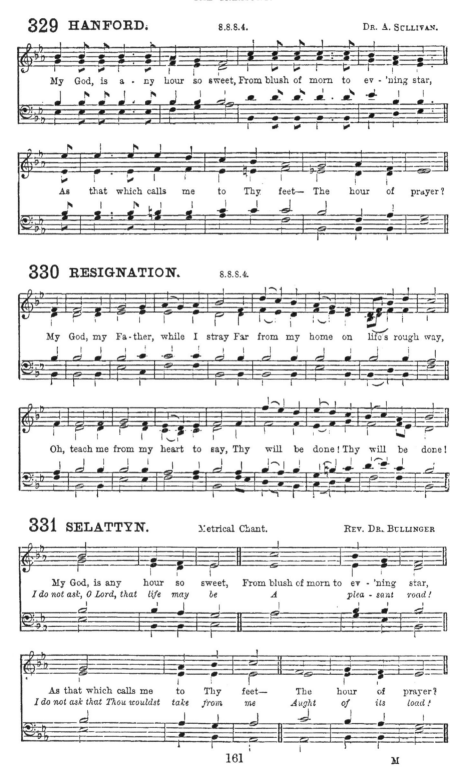

329 HANFORD. 8.8.8.4. DR. A. SULLIVAN.

My God, is a - ny hour so sweet, From blush of morn to ev - 'ning star,

As that which calls me to Thy feet— The hour of prayer?

330 RESIGNATION. 8.8.8.4.

My God, my Fa - ther, while I stray Far from my home on life's rough way,

Oh, teach me from my heart to say, Thy will be done! Thy will be done!

331 SELATTYN. Metrical Chant. REV. DR. BULLINGER.

My God, is any hour so sweet, From blush of morn to ev - 'ning star,
I do not ask, O Lord, that life may be A plea - sant road!

As that which calls me to Thy feet— The hour of prayer?
I do not ask that Thou wouldst take from me Aught of its load!

332 SHOREHAM. 8.8.8.4. REV. DR. J. B. DYKES. From "Congregational Church Music."

My God, my Fa-ther, while I stray Far from my home on life's rough way,

Oh, teach me from my heart to say, Thy will be done!

333 AGNUS DEI. 8.8.8.6. REV. WM. BLOW.

Just as I am— with-out one plea, But that Thy blood was shed for me,

And that Thou bidd'st me come to Thee, O Lamb of God, I come!

334 JUST AS I AM. 8.8.8.6.

Just as I am— with-out one plea, But that Thy blood was shed for me,

And that Thou bidd'st me come to Thee, O Lamb of God, I come!

335 HUMILITY.   8.8.8.6.   WILLIAM BEST.

The Sab-bath-day has reached its close, Yet, Sa - viour, ere I seek re - pose,

pp rall.

Grant me the peace Thy love be - stows: Smile on my ev -'ning hour.

336 CÉLESTE.   8.8.8.8., with Chorus.

We speak of the realms of the blest, That coun - try so bright and so fair;

And oft are its glo - ries con - fessed— But what must it be to be there?

CHORUS.

But what, but what, But what must it be to be there? And

oft are its glo - ries con - fessed— But what must it be to be there?

337 ST. MATTHIAS. 8.8.8.8.8.8. Dr. W. H. Monk. From "Hymns Ancient and Modern," by per.

Sweet Sa-viour, bless us ere we go; Thy word in-to our minds in-stil;

And make our luke-warm hearts to glow With low-ly love and fer-vent will.

Thro' life's long day and death's dark night, O gen-tle Je-sus, be our light!

338 STELLA. 8.8.8.8.8.8.

Sweet Sa-viour, bless us ere we go; Thy word in-to our minds in-stil;

And make our luke-warm hearts to glow With low-ly love and fer-vent will.

Thro' life's long day and death's dark night, O gen-tle Je-sus, be our light!

339 MONMOUTH. 888.888.

I'll praise my Ma - ker with my breath, And when my voice is lost in death, Praise

shall em - ploy my no-bler pow'rs; My days of praise shall ne'er be past While

life...... and thought and be - ing last,......Or im - mor - tal - i - ty en - dures.

340 FRIBURG. 9.8.9.8.8.8. F. SILCHER.

Bap - tized in - to Thy name, most ho - ly: O Fa - ther, Son, and Ho - ly Ghost:

I claim a place, tho' weak and low - ly, A - mong Thy seed, Thy chos - en host;

Bur - ied with Christ, and dead to sin, Thy Spi - rit now shall dwell with - in.

341 THERE'S A BEAUTIFUL LAND ON HIGH.

8.8.6.5.8., with Chorus.

W. U. BUTCHER.

There's a beau - ti -ful land on high, To its glo - ries I fain would fly;

When by sorrows press'd down I long for my crown In that beau - ti - ful land on high.

CHORUS. *Cheerfully.*

In that beau - ti - ful land I'll be From earth and its cares set free; My

Je - sus is there, He's gone to pre - pare A place in that land for me.

342 OH, THINK OF THE HOME.

8.9.9.9., with Chorus.

J. C. O'KANE.

Oh, think of the home o - ver there, By the side of the riv - er of light,

Where the saints, all im - mor - tal and fair, Are robed in their gar - ments of white.

343 COMPASSION. 9.7.9.7.9.9., Irregular. FOUNTAIN MEEN

1. There were nine-ty and nine that safe-ly lay In the shel-ter of the fold;
2. "Lord, Thou hast here Thy ninety and nine, Are they not e-nough for Thee?"
3. But none of the ran-som'd ev-er knew How deep were the wa-ters crossed;
4. "Lord, whence are those blood-drops all the way That mark out the mountain's track?"
5. And all thro' the mountains, thun-der-riv'n, And up from the rock-y steep,

But one was out on the hills a-way, Far off from the gates of gold, A-
But the Shepherd made answer: "This of Mine Has wandered a-way from Me; And al-
Nor how dark was the night that the Lord pass'd thro' Ere He found His sheep that was lost:
"They were shed for one who had gone a-stray Ere the Shepherd could bring him back." "Lord,
There rose a cry to the gate of heav'n, "Rejoice! I have found My sheep!" And the

- way on the mountains wild and bare, A-way from the ten-der Shep-herd's care.
- though the road be rough and steep, I go to the desert to find My sheep."
Out in the desert He heard its cry, Sick and helpless, and rea-dy to die
whence are Thy hands so rent and torn?" "They are pierc'd to-night by ma-ny a thorn."
an-gels echoed a-round the throne. "Re-joice! for the Lord brings back His own!"

344 A CROWD FILLS THE COURT. J. COURTNAY. By permission of
the Sunday School Union.
9.8.9.8., Dble.

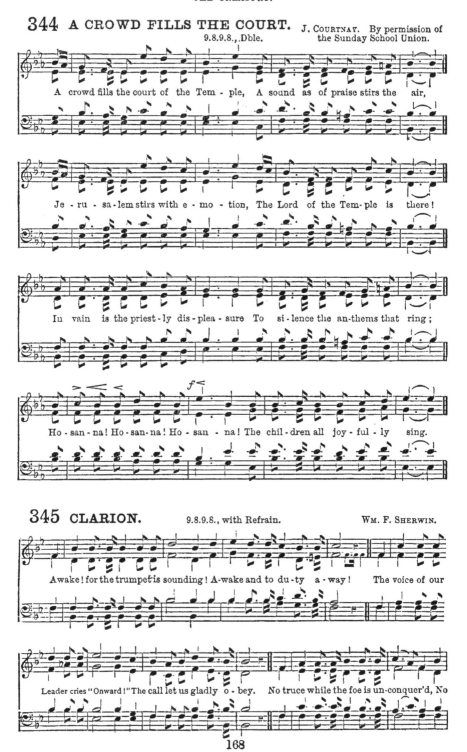

A crowd fills the court of the Tem - ple, A sound as of praise stirs the air,

Je - ru - sa - lem stirs with e - mo - tion, The Lord of the Tem - ple is there!

In vain is the priest - ly dis - plea - sure To si - lence the an - thems that ring;

Ho - san - na! Ho - san - na! Ho - san - na! The chil - dren all joy - ful - ly sing.

345 CLARION. 9.8.9.8., with Refrain. WM. F. SHERWIN.

Awake! for the trumpet is sounding! A - wake and to du - ty a - way! The voice of our

Leader cries "Onward!" The call let us gladly o - bey. No truce while the foe is un - conquer'd, No

346 THE BETTER LAND.

9.10.9.9.10.10.6., Irregular.

MISS DAVIS. By permission of
MESSRS. METZLER & CO.

lay-ing our ar-mour down! No peace till the battle is end-ed, And vic-to-ry wins the crown!

1. "I hear thee speak of a bet-ter land, Thou call'st its children a hap-py band;
2. "Is it where the feather-y palm-trees rise, And the date grows ripe under sunny skies? Or
3. "Is it far a-way in some re-gion old, Where the riv-ers wander o'er sands of gold? Where the
4. "Eye hath not seen it, my gen-tle boy! Ear hath not heard its deep songs of joy!

Mo-ther, oh, where is that ra-diant shore? Shall we not seek it and weep no more?
'midst the green is-lands in glit-ter-ing seas, Where frag-rant fo-rests perfume the breeze,
burn-ing rays of the ru-by shine, And the diamond lights up the se-cret mine,
Dreams cannot pic-ture a world so fair— Sorrow and death may not en-ter there:

Is it where the flow'r of the o-range blows, And the fire-flies glance thro' the myr-tle boughs?"
And strange bright birds, on their star-ry wings Bear the rich hues of all glorious things?"
And the pearl gleams forth from the cor-al strand, Is it there, sweet mother, that bet-ter land?"
Time doth not breathe in its fade-less bloom, For be-yond the clouds and be-yond the tomb,

"Not there, not there, my child! Not there, not there, my child!"
"Not there, not there, my child! Not there, not there, my child!"
"Not there, not there, my child! Not there, not there, my child!"
It is there, it is there, my child! It is there, it is there, my child!"

347 SOWING THE SEED. 9.9.9.9.7.7., Irregular, with Refrain.

P. P. BLISS

time............ or e · ter · · · · · ni · ty,...............

-ter · ni · ty, Ga · th.ered in time or e · ter · ni · ty,

Sure,............... ah! yes, sure............ will the har · · · vest be.

Sure, ah! yes, sure will the har · vest be, will the har · vest, the har · vest be.

348 MARCH OF LIFE. 10.8.10.8., Dble., with Refrain. W. F. SHERWIN.

In the march of life, thro' the toil and strife Of the wind·ing path be - fore us,

FINE.

We have nought to fear with a Sa·viour near, And His ban·ner wav·ing o'er us.

If the tem·pest rise in the dark·'ning skies, We will yield to no re·pin·ing;

D.C. al fine.

Though the storm roar loud, thro' the rift - ed cloud There's a gold - en sun·beam shin - ing.

349 THOU DIDST LEAVE THY THRONE.

10.8.10.8., Irregular, with Refrain.

1. Thou didst leave Thy throne and Thy King-ly crown, When Thou cam-est to earth for
2. Hea-ven's arch-es rang when the an-gels sang, Pro-claim-ing Thy Roy-al de-
3. The fox-es found rest, and the birds had their nest In the shade of the for-est
4. Thou cam-est, O Lord, with the liv-ing Word That should set Thy peo-ple
5. When heaven's arches shall ring, and her choirs shall sing At Thy com-ing to vic-to-

1. me; But in Beth-le-hem's home was there found no room For Thy
2. -gree; But of low-ly birth cam'st Thou, Lord, on earth, And in
3. tree; But Thy couch was the sod, O Thou Son of God, In the
4. free; But with mock-ing scorn, and with crown of thorn, They
5. -ry, Let Thy voice call me home, say-ing, "Yet there is room, There is

REFRAIN.

1. ho-ly Na-ti-vi-ty:
2. great hu-mi-li-ty:
3. de-serts of Ga-li-lee: } 1.2.3. Oh, come to my heart, Lord
4. bore Thee to Cal-va-ry; 4. Oh, come to my heart, Lord
5. room at My side for thee!" 5. And my heart shall re-joice, Lord

1.2.3. Je-sus! There is room in my heart for Thee; Oh,
4. Je-sus! Thy cross is my on-ly plea; Oh,
5. Je-sus! When Thou com-est and call-est for me; And my

1.2.3. come to my heart, Lord Je-sus, come, There is room in my heart for Thee.
4. come to my heart, Lord Je-sus, come, Thy cross is my on-ly plea.
5. heart shall re-joice, Lord Je-sus! When Thou com-est and call-est for me.

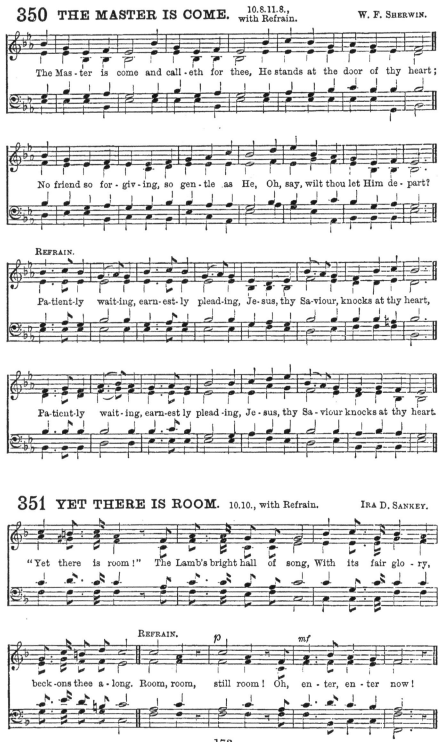

350 THE MASTER IS COME. 10.8.11.8., with Refrain. W. F. SHERWIN.

The Mas-ter is come and call-eth for thee, He stands at the door of thy heart;

No friend so for-giv-ing, so gen-tle as He, Oh, say, wilt thou let Him de-part?

REFRAIN.

Pa-tient-ly wait-ing, earn-est-ly plead-ing, Je-sus, thy Sa-viour, knocks at thy heart,

Pa-tient-ly wait-ing, earn-est-ly plead-ing, Je-sus, thy Sa-viour knocks at thy heart.

351 YET THERE IS ROOM. 10.10., with Refrain. IRA D. SANKEY.

"Yet there is room!" The Lamb's bright hall of song, With its fair glo-ry,

REFRAIN. p mf

beck-ons thee a-long. Room, room, still room! Oh, en-ter, en-ter now!

173

352 SERAPHIM. 10.9.10.9.10.10.8.10.10.8. SCHUBERT.

Glo - ry, glo - ry to God in the high-est! An - gels in cho - rus

joy - ful - ly cry; Glo - ry, glo - ry to God in the high-est! Trembling and weak our

voi - ces re - ply. Fain would we e - cho their an - them a - bove,

Fain would we sing to the Foun-tain of love, Glo - ry to God in the high - est!

What though but fee - bly our ac - cents a - rise, Deign - ing to heark - en, He

bends from the skies, Glo - ry to God in the high - est!

353 LEAD ME TO JESUS. 10.9.10.9., with Refrain.

Lead me to Je-sus, lead me to Je-sus; Help me to love Him, teach me to pray:

He is my Sa-viour, I would be-lieve Him; I would be like Him—show me the way.

CHORUS. *pp*   *cres.*   *rall.*

Quickly haste and come where happy children meet, Hither come and sing the Saviour's praises sweet;

tempo.   *f*

Rest from thy plea-sures, rest from thy play, Come to our meet-ing, come a-way.

354 ELLERS.   10.10.10.10.   DR. E. J. HOPKINS.

The day was done; be-side the sul-try shore The cool-ing sha-dows kissed the rest-less sea;

The words of won-drous wis-dom now were o'er That made thy waves so sa-cred, Ga-li-lee!

355 EVENTIDE. 10.10.10.10. Dr. W. H. Monk. From "Hymns Ancient and Modern," by per.

A-bide with me! fast falls the e-ven-tide: The darkness thick-ens: Lord, with me a-bide!

When o-ther help-ers fail and comforts flee, Help of the help-less, O a-bide with me!

356 PAX DEI. 10.10.10.10. Rev. Dr. J. B. Dykes. From "Hymns Ancient and Modern," by per.

Sa-viour, a-gain to Thy dear name we raise, With one ac-

-cord, our part-ing hymn of praise; We stand to bless Thee

ere our wor-ship cease, Then, low-ly kneel-ing, wait Thy word of peace.

357 ST. AGNES. 10.10.10.10. J. Langran.

Wea-ry of earth and la-den with my sin, I look at heaven and long to en-ter in;

176

But there no e . vil thing may find a home : And yet I hear a voice that bids me come.

358 TOULON.   10.10.10.10.   C. Goudimel.

Teach me to live! 'tis eas-ier far to die—Gen-tly and si-lent-ly to pass a-way—

On earth's long night to close the hea-vy eye, And wak-en in the glo-rious realms of day.

359 AYLESBURY.   10.10.10.10.4.   W. C. Filby.

p

It pass-eth know-ledge, that dear love of Thine, My Je-sus, Sa-viour;

cres. *p*

yet this soul of mine Would of Thy love, in all its breadth and length, Its

cres. *f*

height and depth, and ev-er-last-ing strength, Know more and more.

360 PATMOS.   10.10.10.10.4.   JOHN ADCOCK.

It pass-eth know-ledge, that dear love of Thine, My Je-sus,
Sa-viour; yet this soul of mine Would of Thy love, in all its breadth and length,
Its height and depth, and ev-er-last-ing strength, Know more and more.

361 THE GOOD OLD WAY.   10.10.10.10., with Chorus.   W. H. DOANE.

We are go-ing forth with our staff in hand, Thro' a de-sert wild in a
stran-gers' land; But our faith is bright and our hope is strong, And the

CHORUS.

Good Old Way is our pil-grim song. 'Tis the Good Old Way, by our

fa - thers trod; 'Tis the way of Life, And it lead - eth un - to God; 'Tis the

on - ly path to the realms of day; We are go - ing home in the Good Old Way.

362 YORKSHIRE.

6 lines, 10s.

Dr. Wainwright.

Chris - tians, a - wake, sa - lute the hap - py morn, Where - on the Sa - viour of man -

- kind was born; Rise to a - dore the mys - te - ry of love, Which hosts of

an - gels chant ed from a - bove: With them the joy - ful ti - dings first be -

- gun, Of God in - car - nate and the Vir - gin's Son.

363 TENTERDEN.   6 lines, 10s.   REV. DR. BULLINGER.

The day is gen-tly sink-ing to a close; Faint-er and yet more faint the sun-light glows: O bright-ness of Thy Fa-ther's glo-ry, Thou E-ter-nal Light of light, be with us now! Where Thou art pre-sent dark-ness can-not be; Mid-night is glo-rious noon, O Lord, with Thee!

364 HANOVER.   10.10.11.11.   DR. CROFT. Arr. V. NOVELLO.

Let children pro-claim Their Saviour and King; To Je-sus' great name Ho-san-nas we sing: Our best a-do-ra-tion To Je-sus we give, Who purchased sal-va-tion For us to re-ceive.

180

365 JOYFULLY, JOYFULLY. 8 lines, 10s. REV. A. D. MERRILL.

Joy-ful-ly, joy-ful-ly, on-ward we move, Bound to the land of bright spi-rits a-bove;

Je-sus our Sa-viour, in mer-cy says Come! Joy-ful-ly, joy-ful-ly, haste to your home.

Soon will our pil-grim-age end here be-low, Soon to the pre-sence of God we shall go;

Then, if to Je-sus our hearts have been given, Joy-ful-ly, joy-ful-ly, rest we in heaven.

366 HOUGHTON. 10.10.11.11. DR. GAUNTLETT. From the "Congregational Psalmist," by per.

O wor-ship the King, all glo-rious a-bove! O grate-ful-ly sing His power and His love;

Our Shield and De-fender, the Ancient of Days, Pavilioned in splendour, and gird-ed with praise.

367 ST. PATRICK. 10.10.11.11. B. Taylor.

O wor-ship the King, all glo-rious a - bove! O grate-ful-ly sing His power and His love;

Our Shield and Defender, the An-cient of Days, Pa-vilioned in splendour, and girded with praise.

368 ON TO THE CONFLICT. 10.13.10.9., with Chorus. W. H. Doane.

On to the con-flict, soldiers, for the right, Arm you with the Spirit's word, and march to the fight;

Truth be your watchword, sound the ring-ing cry, Vic - to - ry, Vic - to - ry, Vic - to - ry!

CHORUS.

Ev - er this the war-cry, Vic-to-ry! Vic - to - ry! Ev - er this the war-cry, Vic - to - ry!

Write it on the ban-ner, waft it on the breeze, Vic - to - ry! Vic-to-ry! Vic - to - ry!

369 ENDSLEIGH. 10s. and 11s., Irregular. ERNEST J. MEAD.

Ho - san - na we sing, like the chil - dren dear In the old - en

days, when the Lord lived here; He blest lit - tle chil - dren, and

smiled on them, When they chant - ed His praise in Je - ru - sa - lem.

Hal - le - lu - jah we sing, like the chil - dren bright, With their

harps of gold and their rai - ment white; As they fol - low their Shep-herd with

lov - ing eyes, Thro' the beau - ti - ful val - leys of Pa - ra - dise.

370 SOUND THE LOUD TIMBREL.

10.11.11.11.12.11.10.11.

Harmonized by A. R.
From the "Methodist Sunday
School Tune Book," by per.

Sound the loud tim-brel o'er E-gypt's dark sea!........... Je-ho-vah hath

triumphed! His peo-ple are free! Sing! for the pride of the ty-rant is bro-ken: His

cha-riots, his horse-men, all splen-did and brave: How vain was their boast-ing! the

Lord hath but spo-ken, And cha-riots and horse-men are sunk in the wave!

Org.

Sound the loud tim-brel o'er E-gypt's dark sea!........... Je-ho-vah hath

triumphed! His peo-ple are free! His peo-ple are free! His peo-ple are free!

Org.

371 HOW SWEET IS THE BIBLE.
11.8.11.8.

JOHN GUEST. By permission.

How sweet is the Bi - ble! how pure is the light That streams from its pa - ges di -

- vine! 'Tis a star that shines clear thro' the gloom of the night, Of jew - els a won - der - ful

mine. 'Tis bread for the hun - gry, 'tis food for the poor, A balm for the wounded and

rall.

sad; 'Tis the gift of a Fa - ther, His likeness is there, And the hearts of His children are glad.

372 BELFIELD.
11.8.11.8.

REV. DR. BULLINGER.

How sweet is the Bi - ble! how pure is the light That streams from its pa - ges di - vine!

'Tis a star that shines clear thro' the gloom of the night, Of jew - els a won - der - ful mine.

373 BEAUTIFUL STREAM.

11.7.11.7., with Chorus

Oh, have you not heard of a beau-ti-ful stream, That flows thro' our Fa-ther's land?

Its wa-ters gleam bright In the hea-ven-ly light, And rip-ple o'er gold-en sand.

REFRAIN.

Oh, seek that beau-ti-ful stream! Oh, seek that beau-ti-ful stream!

Its wa-ters so free Are flow-ing for thee: Oh, seek that beau-ti-ful stream!

374 RING THE BELLS OF HEAVEN.

11.9.11.9., with Chorus.

G. F. Root.

Ring the bells of hea-ven! there is joy to-day For a soul re-turn-ing from the wild!

See! the Fa-ther meets him out up-on the way, Wel-com-ing His wea-ry, wand'ring child.

CHORUS.

Glo - ry! glo - ry! how the an - gels sing! Glo - ry! glo - ry! how the loud harps ring!

'Tis the ransomed ar - my, like a migh -ty sea, Peal-ing forth the anthem of the free.

375 A CROWN FOR THE YOUNG.

11.9.12.9., with Refrain.

REV. A. A. GRALEY.

I know there's a crown for the saints of renown, And for saints whose good deeds are unsung;

But, oh say, is it true, if their days are but few, That a crown is laid up for the young?

REFRAIN.

Yes, yes, yes; I know there's a crown for the young: If their

lives dai - ly prove that the Sa-viour they love, I know there's a crown for the young.

376 ATHENS. 11.8 11.9.11.9.11.9. Greek Melody.

I think when I read that sweet sto - ry of old, When Je - sus was here a - mong men, How He called lit - tle chil - dren as lambs to His fold, I should like to have been with them then. I wish that His hand had been placed on my head, That His arms had been thrown a - round me; And that I might have seen His kind look when He said, "Let the lit - tle ones come un - to Me."

377 EPIPHANY HYMN. 11.10.11.10.

Rev. J. F. Thrupp.

Brightest and best of the sons of the morning ! Dawn on our darkness and lend us Thine aid ;

Star of the East ! the ho - ri - zon a - dorn-ing, Guide where our in-fant Re-deem-er is laid.

378 MARLBOROUGH. 11.10.11.10.

Oh ! for the peace that flow-eth as a riv - er, Mak-ing life's de-sert places bloom and smile ;

Oh ! for the faith to grasp heaven's light for ev - er, A-mid the shadows of earth's "little while."

379 SALOME. 11.11.

Sweet spi - ces they brought on their star - light - ed way,

And came to the grave by the dawn - ing of day.

380 HARK! HARK, MY SOUL. 11.10.11.10.9.10.

Hark! hark, my soul, an - gel - ic songs are swell - ing O'er earth's green
fields and o - cean's wave-beat shore: How sweet the truth those
bless - ed strains are tell - ing, Of that new life when sin shall be no more.
Au - gels of Je - sus, an - gels of light, Sing - ing to wel - come the
pil - grims of the night! Sing - ing to wel - come the pil - grims of the night!

381 PILGRIMS. 11.10.11.10.9.10. H. Smart. From "Hymns Ancient and Modern," by per.

Hark! hark, my soul, an - gel - ic songs are swell - ing O'er earth's green fields and

o-cean's wave-beat shore : How sweet the truth those bless-ed strains are tell-ing,

Of that new life when sin shall be no more. An-gels of Je-sus,

an-gels of light, Sing-ing to wel-come the pil-grims of the night!

382 REJOICE AND BE GLAD. 11.11., with Chorus. English Air.

Re-joice and be glad! The Re-deem-er has come! Go look on His

CHORUS.

cra-dle, His cross, and His tomb! Sound His prais-es, tell the sto-ry of

Him who was slain; Sound His prais-es, tell with glad-ness He liv-eth a-gain!

383 WE ARE MARCHING ON.

11.11.11.7., Dble., with Refrain.

W. B. BRADBURY.

384 OLDENBURG. *   11.11.11.11.   T. Selle.

The Bi - ble! the Bi - ble! more pre - cious than gold, The hopes and the

glo - ries its pa - ges un - fold; It speaks of a Sa - viour, and

tells of His love; It shows us the way to the man - sions a - bove.

385 REST.   11.11:11.11.   J. White. From the "Sacred Melodist," by per.

O hea - ven, sweet hea - ven, The home of the blest, Where hearts, once in

trou - ble, Are ev - er at rest; Where eyes that could see not Re-

- joice in the light, And beg - gars, made prin - ces, Are walk - ing in white.

O

386 ST. LUKE.   11.11.11.11.

Draw near-er, my Sa-viour, In mer-cy be-hold, And keep me for ev-er, Safe, safe in the fold: More watch-ful and trust-ing, Oh, help me to be, More ho-ly, dear Sa-viour, More faith-ful to Thee.

387 FOUNDATION.*   11.11.11.11.   FATHER BERNARD.

How firm a foun-da-tion, ye saints of the Lord, Is laid for your faith in His ex-cel-lent word! What more can He say than to you He hath said—You who un-to Je-sus for re-fuge have fled?

388. DEAR SAVIOUR, WE GATHER.

11.11.11.11., with Chorus.

W. B. BRADBURY

Dear Sa - viour, we ga - ther our tri - bute to bring, The breath-ings of

love, like blos - soms of spring; Our gra - cious Re - deem - er! we

grate - ful - ly raise Our hearts and our voi - ces in hymn - ing Thy praise

CHORUS.

Hal - le - lu - jah! Hal - le - lu - jah! Ho -

Hal - le - lu - jah! Hal - le - lu - jah!

- san - na in the high - est! Hal - le - lu - jah! Hal - le -

Hal - le - lu - jah!

- lu - jah! Ho - san - na to the Lord!......

Hal - le - lu - jah!

389 HOME, SWEET HOME.

11.11.11.11., with Chorus.

From "Gems of Song Music," by permission.

Be-yond the dark riv-er a land I be-hold, A coun-try all fair, and a

ci-ty of gold; Sweet home: where the bur-dened and wea-ry find rest, The

home of my Fa-ther—the land of the blest.   CHORUS.   Home, home,

sweet, sweet home, The home of my Fa-ther—there's no place like home.

390 I HAVE A SAVIOUR. 11.11.11.11., with Chorus.

IRA D. SANKEY.

I have a Sa-viour, He's plead-ing in glo-ry, A dear lov-ing Sa-viour tho'

earth-friends be few, And now He is watch-ing in ten-der-ness o'er me, And

391 O CHRISTIAN, AWAKE.

11.11.11.11., with Chorus.

By permission of the Sunday School Union.

O Chris-tian, a - wake! for the strife is at hand, With hel - met and

shield, and a sword in thy hand; To meet the bold tempt - er, go,

fear - less - ly go! And stand like the brave with thy face to the foe.

Stand like the brave, Stand like the brave, Stand like the brave with thy face to the foe.

197

392 LOVE ONE ANOTHER. 11.11.11.11.

P. P. BLISS.

This is My com-mand-ment, That ye love one an - o - ther, That ye love one an -

Verses 2 and 3 begin here.

FINE.

- o - ther, As I have lov - ed you. Bless-ed words of Je - sus we have heard to -

Quicker.

- day, Sa-viour, by Thy Spi - rit, help us to o - bey: May Thy love u - nite us

to the liv - ing Vine! May our hearts, en - light-ened, glow with love di - vine!

393 SO NEAR TO THE KINGDOM.

11.11.11.11., with Chorus.

R. LOWRY.

So near to the King-dom! yet what dost thou lack? So near to the

King-dom! what keep-eth thee back? Re-nounce ev - 'ry i - dol, tho' dear it may

198

CHORUS.

be, And come to the Sa-viour now plead-ing with thee. Plead - - ing with

Plead-ing with thee,

thee,............ .... The Sa-viour is plead-ing, is plead-ing with thee.

Plead - ing with thee,

394 ERASTUS.   6 lines, 11.   H. F. HEMY. From the "Crown of Jesus," by permission of MR. H. C. HEMY, Newcastle-on-Tyne

How sweet is the Sab-bath, a morn-ing of rest, The day of the week I love

dear-est and best! This morn-ing my Sa-viour a-rose from the tomb, And

broke all the fet-ters of sin and its doom. How sweet is the Sab-bath, a

morn-ing of rest, The day of the week I love dear-est and best!

395 COLUMBIA. 11.11.11.11., with Chorus. Re-arranged by C. DARNTON.

March on-ward, march on-ward, our ban-ner of light Is wav-ing be-

-fore us ma-jes-tic and bright; March on-ward thro' tri-al, temp-

ta-tion, and strife, No rest from the con-flict—the bat-tle of life.

CHORUS.

Press for-ward, look up-ward, be strong in the Lord, Our hope in His

mer-cy, our trust in His word; Press for-ward, look up-ward, march

home-ward, and sing, All glo-ry to Je-sus, to Je-sus our King.

396 ST. FAITH.   6 lines, 11s.

Our lov-ing Re-deem-er, we trust in Thy word, The word which of old called the

chil-dren to Thee; Its tones all so ten-der, with joy we have heard,—For-

-bid not the lambs who would come un-to Me, For-bid not the lambs who would

come un-to Me. We come, oh, we come! Thou wilt wel-come us home; The

rest of our souls on Thy bo-som shall be; We come, oh, we come! Thou wilt

wel-come us home; The rest of our souls on Thy bo-som shall be.

397 NICÆA. 11.12.12.10. REV. DR. J. B. DYKES. From "Hymns Ancient and Modern," by per.

Ho - ly, Ho - ly, Ho - ly! Lord God Al - migh - ty! Grate - ful - ly a -

- dor - ing, our song shall rise to Thee! Ho - ly, Ho - ly, Ho - ly!

Mer - ci - ful and Migh - ty! God in Three Per - sons, Bless - ed Tri - ni - ty!

398 IN THE HIGHWAYS. 12.7.12.7., with Chorus. W. H. DOANE.

In the high-ways and hedg-es go seek for the lost, Ga - ther them in - to the

fold— Was the earn - est com - mand that our Sa - viour di - vine

CHORUS.

Taught His dis - ci - ples of old. Urge them to come, show them the way,

Ten - der - ly, lov - ing - ly, bring them to - day; Urge them to come,

why should they roam? Bring them a - long to our dear Sab - bath Home.

399 THERE'S A BEAUTIFUL LAND.

11.8.11.8., with Chorus.

W. W. JOHNSON.
By permission of the Sunday
School Union.

There's a beau - ti - ful land where the rains nev - er beat, And the keen east winds nev - er blow:

And they feel not the glow of the sum - mer heat, Nor the chill of the win - ter snow.

CHORUS.

'Tis hea - ven, sweet hea - ven, that beau - ti - ful land; There is

no-thing on earth Of true beau - ty or worth To com-pare with the beau - ti - ful land.

400 THERE IS LIFE FOR A LOOK.

11.9.11.9., with Chorus.

E. G. TAYLOR.

There is life for a look at the Cru - ci - fied One, There is life at this
mo-ment for thee; Then look, sin-ner, look un - to Him and be saved, Un-to
Him who was nailed to the tree. Look! look! look and live! There is
life for a look at the Cru - ci - fied One, There is life at this mo-ment for thee.

CHORUS.

401 THERE IS LIFE FOR A LOOK.

11.9.11.9., with Chorus.

From "Hymns of Salvation."

{ There is life for a look at the Cru - ci - fied One, There is life at this mo-ment for thee; }
{ Then look, sin-ner, look un-to Him and be saved, Un-to Him who was nailed to the tree. }

Look un - to Him, look un - to Him, Un - to Him who was nailed to the tree!

402 EMS. 13.11.13.12. German Chorale.

Thou art gone to the grave, But we will not de-plore thee, Tho' sor-rows and

dark-ness En-com-pass the tomb; The Sa-viour has passed Thro' its

por-tals be-fore thee, And the lamp of His love Is thy guide thro' the gloom.

403 SALEM. 13.13.8.8.11.

When mo-thers of Sa-lem their children brought to Je-sus, The stern dis-ci-ples

drove them back, and bade them de-part; But Je-sus saw them ere they fled, And

sweet-ly smil-ing, kind-ly said, Suf-fer lit-tle chil-dren to come un-to Me.

404

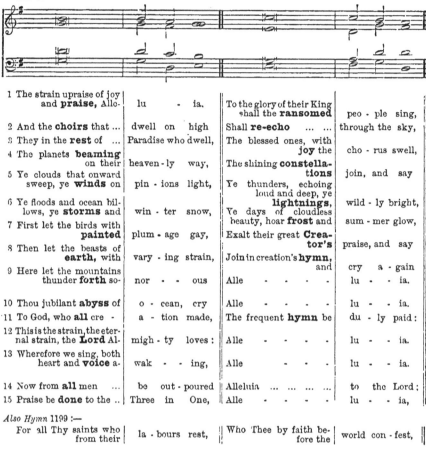

1	The strain upraise of joy and **praise**, Allo-	lu - ia.	To the glory of their King shall the **ransomed**	peo - ple sing,
2	And the **choirs** that ...	dwell on high	Shall **re-echo**	through the sky,
3	They in the **rest** of ...	Paradise who dwell,	The blessed ones, with **joy** the	cho - rus swell,
4	The planets **beaming** on their	heaven - ly way,	The shining **constella-tions**	join, and say
5	Ye clouds that onward sweep, ye **winds** on	pin - ions light,	Ye thunders, echoing loud and deep, ye **lightnings**,	wild - ly bright,
6	Ye floods and ocean bil-lows, ye **storms** and	win - ter snow,	Ye days of cloudless beauty, hoar **frost** and	sum - mer glow,
7	First let the birds with **painted**	plum - age gay,	Exalt their great **Crea-tor's**	praise, and say
8	Then let the beasts of **earth**, with	vary - ing strain,	Join in creation's **hymn**, and	cry a - gain
9	Here let the mountains thunder **forth** so-	nor - - ous	Alle - - - -	lu - - ia.
10	Thou jubilant **abyss** of	o - cean, cry	Alle - - - -	lu - - ia.
11	To God, who **all** cre -	a - tion made,	The frequent **hymn** be	du - ly paid:
12	This is the strain, the eter-nal strain, the **Lord** Al-	migh - ty loves:	Alle - - - -	lu - - ia.
13	Wherefore we sing, both heart and **voice** a-	wak - - ing,	Alle - - - -	lu - - ia.
14	Now from **all** men ...	be out - poured	Alleluia	to the Lord:
15	Praise be **done** to the ..	Three in One,	Alle - - - -	lu - - ia,

Also Hymn 1199 :—

For all Thy saints who from their	la - bours rest,	Who Thee by faith be-fore the	world con - fest,

405 SANCTUS.

CAMIDGE.

Slow. *mf* *cres.* *f*

Ho - ly, Ho - ly, Ho - ly, Lord God of Hosts, heaven and earth are

mf *cres.* *f*

full of Thy glo - ry Glo - ry be to Thee, O Lord most High.

Org.

TROYTE, No. 2.

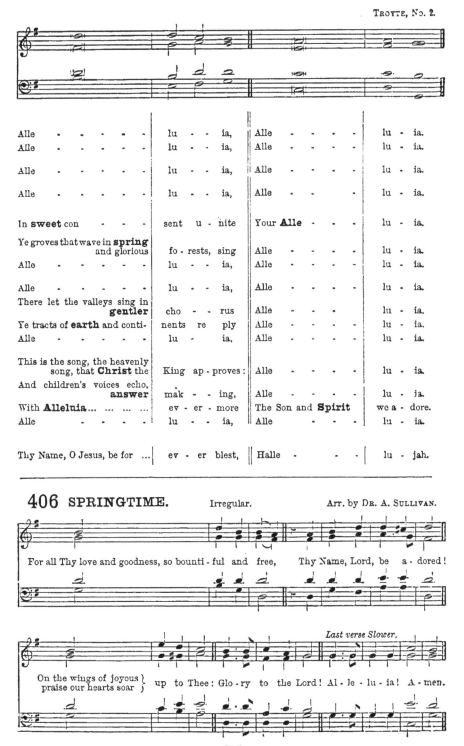

Alle . . . . . lu - - ia, Alle . - . - lu - ia.
Alle . . . . . lu - - ia, Alle - . . - lu - ia.

Alle . . . . - lu - - ia, Alle - . - - lu - ia.

Alle . . . . - lu - - ia, Alle - . - lu - ia.

In **sweet** con - - - sent u - nite Your **Alle** - - - lu - ia.

Ye groves that wave in **spring**
and glorious fo - rests, sing Alle . - . - lu - ia.
Alle . . . . - lu - - ia, Alle - . - - lu - ia.

Alle . . . - - lu - - ia, Alle - . - - lu - ia.
There let the valleys sing in
gentler cho - - rus Alle - . . lu - ia.
Ye tracts of **earth** and conti- nents re ply Alle - . - lu - ia.
Alle - - - - lu - ia, Alle - . - - lu - ia.

This is the song, the heavenly
song, that **Christ** the King ap - proves: Alle - . - lu - ia.
And children's voices echo,
answer mak - - ing, Alle - . - - lu - ia.
With **Alleluia** ... ... ev - er - more The Son and **Spirit** we a - dore.
Alle . - . . - lu - - ia, Alle - . - lu - ia.

Thy Name, O Jesus, be for ... ev - er blest, ‖ Halle - . - lu - jah.

---

406 SPRINGTIME. Irregular. Arr. by Dr. A. Sullivan.

For all Thy love and goodness, so bounti - ful and free, Thy Name, Lord, be a - dored!

Last verse Slower.

On the wings of joyous } up to Thee: Glo - ry to the Lord! Al - le - lu - ia! A - men.
praise our hearts soar }

DOUBLE CHANTS.

407   ALCOCK.

408   ALDRICH.

409   DR. BOYCE.

410   DR. CROTCH.

411   DR. DUPUIS.

412   From HANDEL.

413 REV. P. HENLEY.

414 R. LANGDON.

415 LORD MORNINGTON.

416 ROBINSON.

METRICAL CHANTS.

417 W. L. REYNOLDS.

"My God, my Father, while I stray."   "By Christ redeemed."

418 TROYTE, No. 1.

"Abide with me fast falls the eventide."

P

419 MUSICAL DREAM.

sin-ner trust in Thee? *Organ only.*

"PROSPECT" † (*Scholars*).

My heart was full; I wept for joy;
  They had not sung in vain;
For God was in that holy place,
  And souls were born again.

The congregation, deeply moved,
  Their earnest prayers renewed;
Another hymn of olden times
  They sang in tones subdued :—

* "ABRIDGE" (*Choir only*).

Organ only.

O for a clos-er walk with God, A calm and heav'n-ly frame; A light to shine up-on the road That leads me to the Lamb! *Organ only.*

"PROSPECT" † (*Scholars*).

The scene was changed; and as I passed
  Along the sea of time,
The Church of God, with one consent,
  From earth's remotest clime,

United at the self-same hour
  In lofty strains to raise
One loud, ecstatic burst of joy,
  One glorious hymn of praise!

Organ only.

Full Swell.

* *In this edition "Abridge" has been substituted for "Warwick." Choirs preferring to continue the use of "Warwick," will find the Music at No.* **58.**

The Congregation to join in singing:—

LORD MORNINGTON.

O for a thousand tongues to sing
 My great Redeemer's praise :
The glories of my God and King,
 The triumph of His grace.

My gracious Master and my God,
 Assist me to proclaim,
And spread through all the earth abroad
 The honours of Thy Name.

Organ only.

"PROSPECT."

Je-sus! the Name that charms our fears, That bids our sor-rows cease ; 'Tis mu-sic

in the sin-ner's ears, 'Tis life, and health, and peace. He speaks—and, list-'ning

to His voice, New life the dead re-ceive; The mournful, bro-ken hearts re-

-joice; The hum-ble poor be-lieve. *Organ only.*

CHANT—"MORNINGTON."
 Glory be to the Father, and to the Son, And to the Holy Ghost ;
 As it was in the beginning, is now, and ever shall be, World without end. Amen.

No. 420, "*I will arise,*" follows No. 422.

421 VITAL SPARK OF HEAVENLY FLAME.

Vi - tal spark of heaven - ly flame, Quit, oh, quit this mor - tal frame!

Trem-bling, hop - ing, ling-'ring, fly - ing— Oh, the pain, the bliss of dy - ing!

Org.

Cease, fond na - ture, cease thy strife, And let me lan - guish in - to life.

Hark! they whis - per, an - gels say, they whis - per, an - gels say, they
Hark! Hark!

whis - per, an - gels say, Hark! they whis - per, an - gels say,
Hark!

Sis - ter spi - rit, come a - way, Sis - ter spi - rit, come a - way.

What is this ab-sorbs me quite, Steals my sen-ses,

shuts my sight, Drowns my spi-rit, draws my breath! Tell me, my

soul, can this be death? Tell me, my soul, can this be death?

Andantino.

The world re-cedes, it dis-ap-pears, Heaven o-pens

on my eyes, my ears With sounds se-ra-phic ring!

Con spirito.

Lend, lend your wings, I mount, I fly! O grave, where is thy vic-to-ry? O

grave, where is thy vic - to - ry? O death, where is thy sting? O grave, where is thy vic - to - ry? O

death, where is thy sting? Lend, lend your wings, I mount, ... I fly! O

grave, where is thy vic - to - ry? thy vic to - ry? O grave, where is thy

vic - to - ry? thy vic - to - ry? O death, where is thy sting? O death, where is thy sting?

Lend, lend your wings, I mount, ... I fly! O grave, where is thy

vic - to - ry? thy vic - to - ry? O death, O death, where is thy sting?

422 TE DEUM LAUDAMUS.

WILLIAM JACKSON.

Org. Bold. f

We praise thee, O God ; we ac - know-ledge thee to be the Lord.

All the earth doth wor -ship thee, the Fa - ther e - ver - last - ing. To thee all an -gels

cry a - loud, the heav'ns and all the pow'rs therein. To thee Che - ru - bin, and

Slower.

Se - ra-phin con-tin - ual - ly do cry, Ho - ly, Ho - ly, Ho - ly, Lord God of

Tempo 1mo.

Sa - baoth ; Heav'n and earth are full of the Ma - jes - ty of thy Glo - ry.

mp The glo - rious com -pa - ny of the A - pos - tles praise thee. The

Org.

good - ly fel-low - ship of the Pro-phets praise thee. The no - - - ble

ar - my of Mar - tyrs praise thee. The ho-ly Church throughout all the world doth ac-know-ledge

thee; The Fa - ther, of an in - fi - nite Ma - jes -ty; Thine hon-our -a - ble,

true, and on - ly Son; Al - so the Ho - ly Ghost, the Com - fort - er.

Thou art the King of Glo - ry, O Christ; Thou art the e - ver-last-ing Son of the

Fa - ther. When thou took'st up- on thee to de - li - ver man: thou didst not ab -hor the

Vir - gin's womb. When thou hadst o - ver -come the sharp - ness of death, Thou didst

o - pen the kingdom of Heav'n to all be - liev - ers. Thou sit-test at the right hand of

God, in the Glo - ry of the Fa - ther. We be-lieve that thou shalt come to

be our Judge. We there -fore pray thee, help thy ser-vants, whom thou hast redeem - ed

with thy pre -cious blood. Make them to be num - bered with thy saints, in glo - ry

e - ver - last - ing. O Lord, save thy peo - ple; and bless thine

he - ri - tage. Go-vern them, and lift them up for e - ver. Day by day we

mag - ni - fy thee; And we wor - ship thy name, e - ver world with-out end. Vouch-

-safe, O Lord, to keep us this day with - out sin. O Lord, have mer - cy up -

- on us, have mer - cy up - on us. O Lord, let thy mer - cy light-

- en up - on us: as our trust, our trust is in thee. O Lord, in thee, in

thee have I trust - ed, let me ne - ver, let me ne - ver be con - foun - ded.

420 I WILL ARISE. *(Arrangement Copyright.)*

I will a - rise, I will a - rise, and go to my Fa - -

- ther, and will say un - to Him, Fa - ther, Fa - -

- ther, I have sin - ned, I have sin - ned, I have sin - ned a - gainst

heaven, and be - fore Thee, and am no more wor - thy to be

call - ed Thy son. I will a - rise, I will a - rise, and

go to my Fa - ther, my Fa - - - - ther.

423 GREENWOOD. S.M. JOSEPH E. SWEETNER.

164. Sweet-ly the ho-ly hymn Breaks on the morn-ing air;

Be-fore the world with smoke is dim We meet to of-fer prayer.

424 ST. AGNES. C.M. REV. J. B. DYKES, MUS.D.

272. Do not I love Thee, O my Lord? Be-hold my heart and see,

And turn each cher-ished i-dol out That dares to ri-val Thee.

425 SYMPATHY. C.M. American.

441. Is there one heart, dear Sa-viour, here That hum-bly seeks for Thee?

Now with Thy pro-mised grace ap-pear, Let each Thy beau-ty see.

426 CASTLE RISING. C.M., Dble.

Rev. F. A. J. Hervey, M.A.
From *The Hymnary*, by per.

149. The ro-seate hues of ear-ly dawn, The bright-ness of the day,

The crim-son of the sun-set sky, How fast they fade a-way!

O for the pearl-y gates of heaven, O for the gold-en floor;

O for the Sun of Right-eous-ness, That set-teth nev-er-more!

434. Come unto Me! the Saviour speaks.

427 ALSACE. L.M.

From Beethoven.

436. It is a thing most won-der-ful, Al-most too won-der-ful to be,

That God's own Son should come from heav'n, And die to save a child like me.

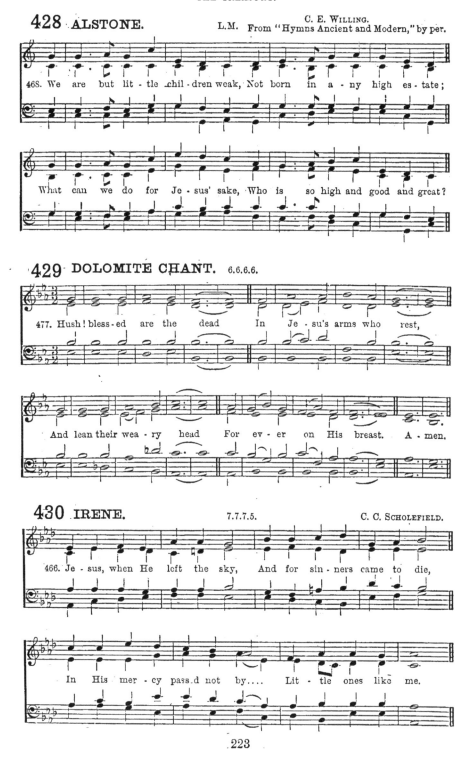

428 ALSTONE. L.M. C. E. WILLING. From "Hymns Ancient and Modern," by per.

468. We are but lit - tle chil - dren weak, Not born in a - ny high es - tate;

What can we do for Je - sus' sake, Who is so high and good and great?

429 DOLOMITE CHANT. 6.6.6.6.

477. Hush! bless - ed are the dead In Je - su's arms who rest,

And lean their wea - ry head For ev - er on His breast. A - men.

430 IRENE. 7.7.7.5. C. C. SCHOLEFIELD.

466. Je - sus, when He left the sky, And for sin - ners came to die,

In His mer - cy pass'd not by.... Lit - tle ones like me.

223

431 LYNDHURST. 6.5.6.5., Dble. By per. of J. NISBET & Co.

167. Now the day is o - ver, Night is draw - ing nigh; Sha - dows of the ev - 'ning Steal a - cross the sky. Now the dark - ness ga - thers, Stars be - gin to peep; Birds and beasts and flow - ers Soon will be a - sleep.

432 MOUNTMELLICK. 6.5.6.5., Dble. T. R. G. JOZÉ, Mus. D.

356. If I come to Je - sus He will make me glad; He will give me plea - sure When my heart is sad. If I come to Je - sus Hap - py I shall be; He is gen - tly call - ing Lit - tle ones like me.

433 PILGRIM SONG. 6.5.6.5., with Chorus. BERTHOLD TOURS.

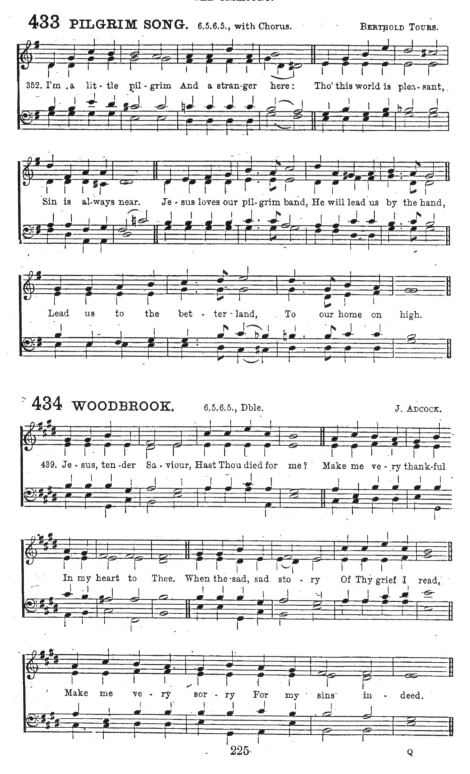

352. I'm a lit-tle pil-grim And a stran-ger here: Tho' this world is plea-sant,

Sin is al-ways near. Je-sus loves our pil-grim band, He will lead us by the hand,

Lead us to the bet-ter land, To our home on high.

434 WOODBROOK. 6.5.6.5., Dble. J. ADCOCK.

439. Je-sus, ten-der Sa-viour, Hast Thou died for me? Make me ve-ry thank-ful

In my heart to Thee. When the sad, sad sto-ry Of Thy grief I read,

Make me ve-ry sor-ry For my sins in-deed.

435 DEVA. 12 lines, 6.5. E. J. HOPKINS, MUS. DOC.

162. Je - sus, bless - ed Sa - viour, Help us now to raise Songs of glad thanks-

- giv - ing, Songs of ho - ly praise. Oh, how kind and gra - cious

Thou hast al - ways been! Oh, how ma - ny blessings Ev - 'ry day has

seen! .... Je - sus, bless - ed Sa - viour, New our prais - es

- hear, For Thy grace and fa - vour Crown-ing all the year.

436 SUMUS TIBI. 12 lines, 6.5. H. ELLIOT BUTTON.

219. Who is on the Lord's side? Who will serve the King? Who will be His

help-ers O - ther lives to bring? - Who will leave the world's side?

Who will face the foe?.... Who is on the Lord's side? Who for

Him will go?.......... By Thy call of mer - cy, By Thy grace di -

- vine,.......... We are on the Lord's side; Sa - viour, we - are Thine.

437 TRINITAS.   7.7.7.5.   CLEMENT H. PERROT.

75. Ev - er bless - ed Trin - i - ty,.... Source of life and pu - ri - ty,....

Hear us, while we lift to Thee Ho - ly chant and psalm......

438 PARKHOLME. 12 lines, 6.5. SAMUEL GEE.

298. For - ward! be our watch - word, Steps and voi - ces joined;
D.C.—For - ward thro' the des - ert, Thro' the toil and fight;

Ped.

FINE.
Ver. 1, 2, 3. | Ver. 4.

Seek the things be - fore us, Not a look be - hind:
Ca - naan lies be - fore us, Zi - on beams with light. light.

Voices in Unison.

Burns the fie - ry pil - lar At our ar - my's head:

ORGAN.

D.C. al Fine.

Who shall dream of shrink - ing, By our Cap - tain led?

439 INVITATION. 6.6.6.6.6.6.6.6.3. F. C. MAKER.

95. Come to the Saviour now! He gen - tly call - eth thee; In true re - pentance bow, Be -

- fore Him bend the knee. He wait-eth to be-stow Sal-va-tion, peace, and love,

True joy on earth be-low, A home in heav'n a-bove. Come, come, come.

440 ROTHBURY.   8.5.8.3.   J. H. MAUNDER.

419. I am trust-ing Thee, Lord Je-sus, Trust-ing on-ly Thee!

Trust-ing Thee for full sal-va-tion, Great...... and free.

441 ELMHURST.   8.8.8.6.   E. DREWETT.

437. Ac-cept-ing, Lord, Thy gra-cious call, Low at Thy feet I hum-bly fall;

Now set me free from Sa-tan's thrall, And let me fol-low Thee.

442 LESLIE. 6.6.6.6.8.8. H. T. LESLIE, Mus.D., by per. From "Tunes and Chants for Home and School."

276. Oft when of God we ask For full - er, hap - pier life,

He sets us some new task, In - vol - ving care and strife:

Is this the boon for which we sought? Has prayer new trou - ble on us brought?

443 SILKSWORTH. 7.5.7.5.7.7. C. J. VINCENT, Jun.

398. Ev - 'ry morn - ing the red sun Ri - ses warm and bright;

But the ev - 'ning com - eth on, And the dark cold night:

There's a bright land far a - way, Where 'tis nev - er - end - ing day.

444 **ALPHA.**   8 lines, 7.6.   HENRY J. LESLIE.

129. Go, when the morning shin - eth; Go, when the noon is bright; Go, when the eve de - clin - eth; Go, in the hush of night; Go, with pure mind and feel - ing, Cast ev - 'ry fear a - way, And, in thy chamber kneel - ing, Do thou in se - cret pray.

445 **CARBROOKE.**   8 lines, 7.6.   J. BOOTH.

416. O Sa-viour, precious Saviour, Whom yet un-seen we love! O Name of might and fa - vour All o-ther names a-bove: We worship Thee, we bless Thee, To Thee a-lone we sing; We praise Thee, and con-fess Thee, Our ho - ly Lord and King!

446 CHENIES.   8 lines, 7.6.   T. R. MATTHEWS.

421. I love my pre-cious Sa-viour, Be-cause He died for me; And if I did not

serve Him, How sin-ful I should be! I know He makes me hap-py, And

hears me when I pray; I'll keep fast hold of Je-sus: The Bi-ble says I may.

447 THE GOLDEN CHAIN. 8 lines, 7.6.

421. I love my pre-cious Sa-viour, Be-cause He died for me; And if I did not

serve Him, How sin-ful I should be! I know He makes me hap-py, And

hears me when I pray; I'll keep fast hold on Je-sus: The Bi-ble says I may.

448 FAIRFORD.   8 lines,—7.6.   From SCHUBERT.

302. Stand up! stand up for Je - sus! Ye sol - diers of the cross; Lift high His roy - al ban - ner, It must not suf - fer loss. From vic - t'ry un - to vic - t'ry His ar - my shall He lead, Till ev - 'ry foe is vanquish'd, And Christ is Lord in - deed.

449 LUX MUNDI.   8 lines, 7.6.   ARTHUR SULLIVAN. From "The Hymnary," by per.

97. To - day Thy mer - cy calls us To wash a - way our sin, How - ev - er great our tres - pass, What-ev - er we have been: How - ev - er long from mer - cy Our hearts have turn'd a - way, Thy pre - cious blood can cleanse us, And make us white to - day.

450 MENDELSSOHN.   8 lines, 7.6.   MENDELSSOHN.

Moderate.

438. I ought to love my Sa·viour; No earth·ly friend can be So

lov·ing, kind, and faith·ful, As He hath been to me. Be·fore my

- fore my lips could ut· · ter

lips........ could ut· · ter His sweet and pre·cious name, Un·

Be·fore my lips could ut·ter Un

- til the pres·ent mo·ment, His love has been the same, Un·

- til the pres·ent mo· · · ·ment, Un·til the pres·ent

dim. His love has been the same.

- til the pres·ent mo·ment, His love............ has been the same.
His love has been the same.

mo· · · ·men_t, His love has been the same.

451 RUTHERFORD.   8 lines, 7.6.

185. The dawn of God's own Sab-bath Breaks o'er the earth a-gain, As some sweet summer morn-ing After a night of pain: It comes as cool-ing show-ers To some dry, parch-ed land, As shade of clus-ter'd palm-trees 'Mid wea-ry wastes of sand.

452 SAVOY CHAPEL.   8 lines, 7.6.   J. B. CALKIN.

409. The hours of day are o-ver, The ev-'ning calls us home; Once more to Thee, O Fa-ther, With thankful hearts we come; For all Thy countless bless-ings We praise Thy ho-ly name, And own Thy love un-chang-ing, Thro' days and years the same.

453 THERE IS A HOLY CITY. 8 lines, 7.6., with Chorus.

473. There is a ho-ly ci-ty, A hap-py world a-bove, Be-

-yond the star-ry re-gions, Built by the God of love.

An ev-er-last-ing tem-ple, And saints ar-rayed in white There

serve the great Re-deem-er, And dwell with Him in light.

CHORUS. *a tempo.*

O home a-bove, O world of love, O ev-er-bless-ed place; A-

236

-bove the sky, At home on high I'll sing of Je-su's grace.

454 ASHBURTON.   6 lines, 7s.   Robert Jackson.

406. Lord, Thy chil-dren guide and keep, As with fee-ble steps they press,

On the path-way rough and steep, Through this wea-ry wil-der-ness.

Ho-ly Je-sus, day by day, Lead us in the nar-row way.

455 GALILEE.   8.7.8.7.   W. H. Jude.

472. Life is re-al, life is earn-est, And the grave is not its goal:

Dust thou art, to dust re-turn-est, Was not spo-ken of the soul.

456 TOURS.   8 lines, 7.6.   BERTHOLD TOURS.
From " The Hymnary," by per.

443. When, His sal - va - tion bring - ing, To Zi - on , Je - sus came,

The chil - dren all stood sing - ing Ho - san - na to His name.

Nor did their zeal of - fend Him, But, as He rode a - long,

He let them still at - tend Him, Well pleased to hear their song.

457 CIVITAS DEI.   7.6.8.6., Dble.   A. J. CALDICOTT, Mus.Bac.

Allegro. cres.   *f*

ORG.   153. Ten thou - sand times ten thou - sand,   In

spark - ling rai - ment white, The ar - mies of the ran - somed saints Throng

up the steeps of light: 'Tis fin-ished! all is finished—Their fight with death and sin;

ff

ritard.

Fling o - pen wide the gold - en gates, And let the vic - tors in. A - men.

* Upper notes may be taken in last verse only.

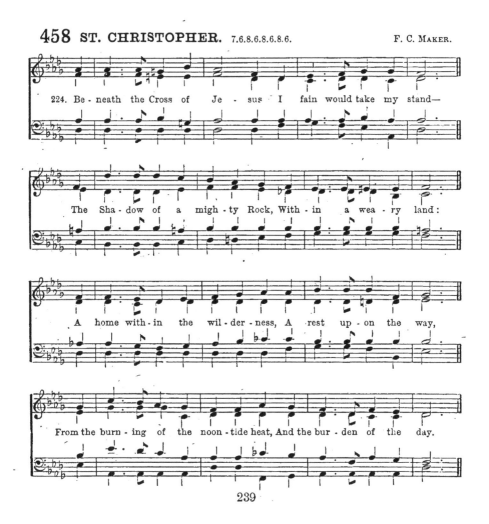

458 ST. CHRISTOPHER. 7.6.8.6.8.6.8.6. F. C. MAKER.

224. Be - neath the Cross of Je - sus I fain would take my stand—

The Sha - dow of a migh -ty Rock, With - in a wea - ry land:

A home with - in the wil - der - ness, A rest up - on the way,

From the burn - ing of the noon - tide heat, And the bur - den of the day.

459 ST. AGNES.   8 lines, 7s.   S. ALICE TUCKER.

487. As the bird in mead - ow fair, Or in lone - ly for - est, sings

Till it fills the sum - mer air,.... And the green-wood sweet - ly rings;

So my heart to Thee would raise, O my God, its song of praise,

That the gloom of night is o'er,.... And I see the sun once more.

460 PATER OMNIUM.   8.8.8.8.8.8.   H. J. E. HOLMES.

404. Lord, from this time we cry to Thee ! Thou of our youth the guide shalt be;

Draw near and take us by the hand, And lead in - to the up - right land !

240

With fire by night and cloud by day, Be with us on our pil-grim way.

461 VENI, DOMINE JESU. 10.8., Irregular.   J. BARNBY.

231. Thou didst leave Thy throne and Thy kingly crown, When Thou cam-est to earth for me :

But in Beth-lehem's home there was found no room For Thy ho - ly Na - tiv - i - ty.

p   *pp*   *rit.*

O come to my heart, Lord Je - sus! There is room in my heart for Thee.

462 IT PASSETH KNOWLEDGE. 10.10.10.10.4.   IRA D. SANKEY.

Moderato. With expression.

119. It pass-eth know-ledge, that dear love of Thine, My Je-sus, Sa-viour ; Yet this soul of mine. Would of Thy

love, in all its breadth and length, Its height, and depth, its ev - er-last-ing strength, Know more and more.

463 BEAUTIFUL STREAM.

11.7.11.7., with Chorus.

J. Baptiste Calkin.
By per. of the Wesleyan Sunday
School Union.

143. Oh, have you not heard of a beau-ti-ful stream, That flows thro' our Fa-ther's land?

Its wa-ters gleam bright In the hea-ven-ly light, And rip-ple o'er gold-en sand.

Oh, seek that beau-ti-ful stream! Oh, seek that beau-ti-ful stream! Its

rit.

wa-ters so free Are flow-ing for thee: Oh, seek that beau-ti-ful stream!

464 HEAVEN, SWEET HEAVEN. P.M.

mf

J. H. Maunder.

140.

Sopranos only.
1. There's a beau-ti-ful land where the rains never beat, And the keen east winds nev-er
Children only.
2. There is ma-ny a child in that beau-ti-ful land; We have brothers and sis-ters
Baritone Solo or Quartet.
3. There was nev-er a tear in that beau-ti-ful land; There was never a mourn-er

blow: And they feel not the glow of the sum-mer heat, Nor the chill of the win-ter's
there; And they dwell with the an-gels a hap-py band, Their glo-ry and joy to
seen; The peo-ple in pure white rai-ment stand In the fields that are al-ways

snow.
share. } 'Tis heav'n, sweet heav'n, that beau-ti-ful, beau-ti-ful land: There's
green.

nothing on earth Of beau-ty or worth To com-pare with the beau-ti-ful land.

FULL CHORUS.

'Tis heav'n, sweet heav'n, that beau-ti-ful, beau-ti-ful land: There's

nothing on earth Of beau-ty or worth To com-pare with the beau ti-ful land.

beau - ty or worth To com - pare with the beau - ti - ful land.

Full Chorus.

'Tis heav'n, sweet heav'n, that beau - ti - ful, beau - ti - ful land: There's

nothing on earth Of beau - ty or worth To com - pare with the beau - ti - ful land.

Full (or Quartet).

5. And if Je - sus shall help me by His grace, There I, too, in light shall stand, And

join in the songs of glo - rious praise, In the fields of the beau - ti - ful

465 HOSANNA WE SING.
10.10.10.10.

J. B. DYKES, Mus. Doc. From
"Hymns Ancient and Modern," by per.

Joyously.

214. Ho-san-na we sing, like the chil-dren dear In the old-en days when the Lord lived here: He blessed lit-tle chil-dren and smiled on them, When they chant-ed His praise in Je-ru-sa-lem.

Hal-le-lu-jah we sing, like the chil-dren bright, With their harps of gold and their rai-ment white, As they fol-low their Shepherd with lov-ing eyes Thro the beau-ti-ful val-leys of Pa-ra-dise.

466 Air—"GOD BLESS THE PRINCE OF WALES."

By Brinley Richards.

(*By arrangement with* Robert Cocks & Co., *the Copyright owners.*)

489. God bless our dear old Eng - land! With cliffs so bold and white, Round

which the an - gry bil - lows So vain - ly roar and fight:

God bless our sons and daugh - ters, And make them pure and brave; By

right - eous - ness the na - tion, O right - eous Fa - ther, save!

God bless our dear old Eng - land! Guard her from ev - 'ry foe; And

grant to all - her child - ren To walk with Thee be - low.

2. God bless our beauteous England !
This cultured garden fair ;
With orchard, meadow, cornfield,
Lovely beyond compare :
Adorn her with the beauties
Of holiness and grace,
These fruits and flowers reflecting,
O Lord, Thy smiling face !

Cho.—God bless our beauteous England !
The land we love so well ;
And grant to all her children
With Thee above to dwell.

3. God bless our grand old England !
With proud historic name ;
And may she yet outrival
Her thousand years of fame :
But chiefly make her steadfast
In godliness and truth,
Wisdom of age uniting
With all the zeal of youth.

Cho.—God bless our grand old England !
So glorious through Thy might ;
And grant to all her children
To battle for the right.

4. God bless our English people !
Brave, loyal, trusty folk ;
Free from all chain of bondage,
Scorning each sinful yoke :
May rich and poor together
Labour and love as one,
A happy royal priesthood—
And so Thy will be done.

Cho.—God bless our dear old England !
And, saved by grace alone,
O grant to all her children
To meet around Thy throne !

GEORGE WILSON, TYPE-MUSIC AND GENERAL PRINTER, 67b, TURNMILL STREET, LONDON. E.C.

Psalms and Hymns

FOR

School and Home.

FOUR HUNDRED AND NINETY APPROPRIATE HYMNS FOR SUNDAY SCHOOLS AND THE FAMILY CIRCLE.

Prepared under the Direction of the Trustees of "Psalms and Hymns,"

Editor, Rev. J. T. WIGNER.

This selection has been specially prepared as the School Edition of "Psalms and Hymns," adapted and enlarged for that purpose. The Hymns are arranged in Five Divisions—1st, Hymns of Worship; 2nd, Anniversaries; 3rd, for Teachers', Prayer, and Special Meetings; 4th, Junior Classes; 5th, Additional Hymns. Text Headings, Authors' Names, &c., are given in the best Editions.

S EDITION, Crown 8vo, Pica.

No. 1. Cloth ... ... 2s. 6d.		No. 4. Calf, limp ... ... 5s. 6d.
No. 2. Sheep ... ... 3s. 0d.		No. 5. Morocco ... ... 6s. 6d.
No. 3. Levant, gilt ... ... 3s. 6d.		No. 6. Morocco, Ex. ... ... 7s. 6d.

T EDITION, F'cap 8vo, Minion.

No. 1. Cloth ... ... 1s. 0d.		No. 3. Calf, limp ... ... 2s. 6d.
No. 2. Levant, gilt ... ... 1s. 8d.		No. 4. Morocco ... ... 3s. 0d.

U EDITION, Royal 32mo, Minion.

No. 1. Cloth, limp ... ... 6d.		No. 3. Levant, gilt ... ... 1s. 0d.
No. 2. Cloth boards ... ... 8d.		No. 4. Calf, limp ... ... 1s. 6d.
	No. 5. Morocco ... ... 2s.	

V EDITION, 32mo, Nonpareil-faced Ruby.

No. 1. Paper cover ... ... 1d.		No. 3. Cloth boards ... ... 4d.
8s. 4d. per 100 nett.		No. 4. Levant, gilt ... ... 10d.
No. 2. Cloth, limp ... ... 2½d.		

W EDITION, 16mo, Pearl.

No. 1. Cloth ... ... 6d.		No. 3. Calf, limp ... ... 2s. 0d.
No. 2. Levant, gilt ... ... 1s. 2d.		No. 4. Morocco ... ... 2s. 6d.

ORDER THUS: 1 doz. V. No. 3, i.e., 12 32mo, at 4d.

25 per cent. allowed on Orders received direct, except the 1d. Edition, which is strictly nett.

PUBLISHED BY THE TRUSTEES, 25, BOUVERIE STREET, E.C.

H. W. PEWTRESS, Secretary, &c., to whom all Cheques, Postal Orders, &c., are to be made payable, crossed "Barclay & Co."

The Treasury

(SCHOOL AND HOME EDITION)

COMPANION TUNE BOOK

TO

"PSALMS AND HYMNS FOR SCHOOL AND HOME,"

466 TUNES, CHANTS, etc.

The Book specifically provides for each hymn in the collection, and concludes with Brinley Richards' National Song, "God Bless the Prince of Wales," set to hymn 489.

Compiled and Edited by Mr. JOSEPH B. MEAD.

Published of uniform size in small 8vo, both in the Staff and Tonic Sol-fa Notations.

No. 13. Cloth Boards, Gold Lettered, Red Edges, Staff or Sol-fa   2s. 6d.

„ 14. Levant, Gilt Edges -   -   -   -   - Staff or Sol-fa   3s· 6d.

„ 15. Half Bound Morocco, Red Edges, very strong, for Choir
use, &c. -   -   -,   -   -   - Staff or Sol-fa   4s. 6d.

Order thus: "1 doz. Treasury No. 13,"
or "1 doz. Treasury No. 13 Sol-fa."

N.B.—The Staff Notation is sent unless the Sol-fa is specifically ordered.

Orders received direct are allowed a Discount of Twenty-five per cent.

A Specimen Copy of any of the above will be sent post free for the published price.

PUBLISHED BY THE TRUSTEES, 25, BOUVERIE STREET, E.C.

H. W. PEWTRESS, Secretary, &c., to whom all Cheques, Postal Orders, &c., are to be made payable, crossed "Barclay & Co."

"Psalms and Hymns,"

Complete with Supplement, contains 1,271 Hymns, with Sanctus and Te Deum. The selection has been made from the best Modern Hymns, as well as from the choicest Hymns of former times, and includes original compositions, expressly written for this book. It is most comprehensive as a Book of Praise for the Sanctuary, and, as it contains many Hymns of a richly experimental character, it is also well adapted for private and social use. It is published in ten different editions, as enumerated below, and in every variety of binding.

It has by far the largest sale of any hymn book of the Denomination, and its general acceptance and approval are evidenced by its widely extended and continually increasing use throughout Great Britain and the Colonies.

The Companion Tune Book, "The Treasury" (Congregational Edition), specifically provides for each hymn in the collection.

A. EDITION. Crown 4to, Double Cols., Pica.

No. 1. Cloth ...	... ... 3s. 0d.	No. 3. Calf	... ...	...	7s. 0d.
No. 2. Levant gilt	... ... 5s. 0d.	No. 4. Morocco...	...	...	8s. 6d.

B. EDITION. Half Imperial 8vo, Single Cols., Pica.

No. 1. Levant gilt	... ... 8s. 0d.	No. 3. Morocco	...	...	11s. 0d.
No. 2. Calf ...	... ... 10s. 0d.	No. 4. Morocco extra ...		...	12s. 6d.

C. EDITION. Crown 8vo, Single Cols., Pica.

No. 1. Cloth ...	... ... 5s. 6d.	No. 3. Calf	... ...	...	9s. 0d.
No. 2. Levant gilt	... ... 7s. 0d.	No. 4. Morocco...	...	...	10s. 0d.
	No. 5. Morocco extra ... ... 12s. 0d.				

D. EDITION. 18mo, Single Cols., Long Primer.

No. 1. Cloth ...	... ... 3s. 6d.	No. 3. Levant gilt	...	...	4s. 6d.
No. 2. Sheep ...	... ... 4s. 0d.	No. 4. Morocco...	...	...	7s. 6d.

E. EDITION. 18mo, Single Cols., Bourgeois.

No. 1. Sheep ...	... ... 3s. 0d.	No. 3. Calf	... ...	...	6s. 6d.
No. 2. Levant gilt	... ... 4s. 6d.	No. 4. Morocco...	...	...	7s. 6d.
	No. 5. Morocco extra ... ... 8s. 6d.				

F. EDITION. Crown 8vo, Double Cols., Brevier.

No. 1. Cloth ...	... ... 2s. 6d.	No. 3. Calf limp	...	...	5s. 0d.
No. 2. Levant gilt	... ... 3s. 6d.	No. 4. Morocco limp ...		...	5s. 6d.
	No. 5. Morocco extra ... ... 6s. 6d.				

Yapp, round corners, in boxes.

No. 6. French Morocco	... 5s. 0d.	No. 7. Grained Persian, red under gold ...		...	7s. 0d.
	No. 8. Morocco, red under gold ... 10s. 6d.				

G. EDITION. Royal 32mo, Single Cols., Brevier.

No. 1. Cloth ...	... ... 2s. 0d.	No. 3. Calf	... ...	...	4s. 0d.
No. 2. Levant gilt	... ... 3s. 0d.	No. 4. Morocco	...	...	5s. 0d.
	No. 5. Morocco extra ... ... 6s. 6d.				

H. EDITION. 32mo, Nonpareil-faced Ruby.

No. 1. Cloth flush	... ... 0s. 6d.	No. 3. Levant gilt	...	...	1s. 2d.
No. 2. Cloth boards	... ... 0s. 8d.	No. 4. Red sheep	...	...	1s. 2d.

J. EDITION. Foolscap 8vo, Double Cols., Pearl.

No. 1. Cloth ...	... ... 2s. 0d.	No. 3. Calf limp	...	...	4s. 6d.
No. 2. Levant gilt	... ... 3s. 0d.	No. 4. Morocco limp ...		...	5s. 6d.
	No. 5. Morocco extra ... ... 6s. 6d.				

K. EDITION. 16mo, Double Cols., Pearl.

No. 1. Cloth ...	... ... 1s. 0d.	No. 3. Red sheep	...	...	1s. 6d.
No. 2. Levant gilt	... ... 1s. 6d.	No. 4. Morocco...	...	...	4s. 0d.
	No. 5. Morocco extra ... ... 4s. 6d.				

Paste grain, padded, round corners, in boxes.

No. 6. Gilt ...	... ... 2s. 6d.	No. 7. Red under gold		...	3s. 0d.
	No. 8. Red with gilt roll ... 3s. 6d.				

Order thus—"1 doz. F. No. 1," *i.e.*, 12 crown 8vo, at 2s. 6d.

PUBLISHED BY THE TRUSTEES, 25, BOUVERIE STREET, E.C.

H. W. PEWTRESS, Secretary, &c., to whom all Cheques, Postal Orders, &c., are to be made payable, crossed "Barclay & Co."

The Treasury

(CONGREGATIONAL EDITION)

COMPANION TUNE BOOK TO "PSALMS & HYMNS."

CONTAINS 613 TUNES AND 45 CHANTS, &c.

Compiled and Edited by Mr. Joseph B. Mead.

The book specifically provides for each hymn in the Collection, and includes 16 Compositions by Sir Arthur S. Sullivan, Mus. Doc., and about 150 by Rev. Sir H. W. Baker, Sir W. Sterndale Bennett, Sir Michael Costa, Sir G. J. Elvey, Sir John Goss, Sir Herbert S. Oakeley, LL.D., Rev. Sir F. A. Gore Ouseley, Bart., Sir John Stainer, Sir Robert P. Stewart, Handel, Purcell, Joseph Barnby, W. H. Callcott, J. Baptiste Calkin, Ch. Gounod, Henry Smart, Berthold Tours, J. Turle, Drs. Boyce, Croft, Dykes (21), Garrett, Gauntlett (24), Hayne, Hiles, Holloway, Hopkins, Howard, Hullah, Jordan, Jozé, Malan, Mann, Monk, Rimbault, Steggall, Wesley, &c.

It concludes with Henry Leslie's arrangement of the "National Anthem," set to hymn 1271, with full Organ Accompaniment as given at the Handel Festivals at the Crystal Palace.

Published of uniform size in Demy 8vo, both in the Staff and Tonic Sol-fa Notations.

No. 1.   Cloth Boards, Gold Lettered, Red Edges, Staff or Sol-fa ...   3s. 6d.
„   2.   Levant, Gilt Edges   ...   .   Staff or Sol-fa ...   4s. 6d.
„   3.   Calf Limp, Gilt Edges ...   .   Staff only   ...   5s. 0d.
„   4.   Half Bound Morocco, Red Edges
         Very Strong, for Choir Use, &c. } Staff or Sol-fa ...   5s. 0d.

Order thus:—"1 doz. Treasury No. 1," or "1 doz. Treasury No. 1 Sol-fa."

N.B.—The Staff Notation is sent unless the Sol-fa is specifically ordered.

ORGAN EDITION. [Super Royal 8vo.

No. 7.   Cloth Boards, Gold Lettered, Red Edges ...   .   6s. 0d.
„   8.   Paste Grain Limp, Gilt Edges   ...   .   7s. 6d.
„   9.   Calf Limp, Gilt Edges   ...   .   10s. 6d.
„ 10.   Half Bound Morocco, Red Edges ...   .   10s. 6d.

This Edition will be found very convenient for use at the Harmonium or Piano in Schools and Families.

Order thus:—"1 doz. Treasury No. 7"—(*i.e.*, 12 Cloth Boards, at 6s.).

Orders received direct are allowed a discount of twenty-five per cent.
A specimen copy of any of the above will be sent post free for the published price.

PUBLISHED BY THE TRUSTEES, 25, BOUVERIE STREET, E.C.
H. W. PEWTRESS, Secretary, &c., to whom all Cheques, Postal Orders, &c., are to be made payable, crossed "Barclay & Co."

Hymns for
YOUNG MEN'S CHRISTIAN ASSOCIATIONS.

Containing 130 Hymns.   Imperial 32mo.

No. I, Cloth Limp, 4d.   No. 2, Cloth Boards, 6d.   No. 3, Levant Gilt, 9d.

Hymn Sheets.

Selected from "Psalms and Hymns," for Anniversary and other Special Services.

Edited by the Rev. J. T. WIGNER.

1.—Chapel Opening and Anniversary Services. 8 pp.
2.—Sunday-School Anniversary Services. 4 pp.
3.—Sunday-School Anniversary Services (No. 2). 4 pp.
4.—Social Gatherings of Church and Congregation. 4 pp.
5.—Baptismal Services. 4 pp.
6.—County Association Meetings. 8 pp.
7.—Missionary Services. 4 pp.
8.—Juvenile Missionary Services. 4 pp.
9.—Evangelistic Services. 8 pp.
10.—Sacred Songs for "Harvest Home." 4 pp.
11.—"In Memoriam" Services. 4 pp.
12.—Communion Services. 4 pp.
13.—Sunday School Anniversary (No. 3). 4 pp.
14.—Musical Dream (with Music). 4 pp.
15.—Hymns for Marriage Services. On folded card. 5s. per 100, nett.

The 8-pp. Sheets, 1s. 9d. per 100 ; the 4-pp. Sheets, 1s.

N. B.—The prices for the Hymn Sheets, 1s. 9d. and 1s. per 100, are nett, and are not subject to any discount.

Specimens of any of these Sheets sent free on application.

The name of any Church or School, or any inscription as "**For the Use of Visitors**," &c., or the name of any recipient of presentation copies, can be stamped in gold on the cover of any of the Hymn or Tune Books.   Prices of lettering on application, giving lettering and number of copies required.

The whole of the Books, &c., advertised in this Prospectus are the property of the Trustees of "PSALMS AND HYMNS," and the profits are annually distributed to Widows and Orphans of Baptist Ministers and Missionaries.   Including the grants made April, 1892, **£16,662** have been devoted to this beneficent object.

PUBLISHED BY THE TRUSTEES, 25, BOUVERIE STREET, E.C.

H. W. PEWTRESS, Secretary, &c., to whom all Cheques, Postal Orders, &c., are to be made payable, crossed "Barclay & Co."

Lightning Source UK Ltd.
Milton Keynes UK
UKHW011511301218
334537UK00012B/1480/P